GOLD

Also by Milton Meltzer

THE AMAZING POTATO:
*A Story in Which the Incas, Conquistadors,
Marie Antoinette, Thomas Jefferson, Wars,
Famines, Immigrants, and French Fries All Play a Part*

THE BILL OF RIGHTS: *How We Got It and What It Means*

VOICES FROM THE CIVIL WAR:
A Documentary History of the Great Conflict

THE AMERICAN REVOLUTIONARIES: *A History in Their Own Words*

RESCUE: *The Story of How Gentiles Saved Jews in the Holocaust*

NEVER TO FORGET: *The Jews of the Holocaust*

AIN'T GONNA STUDY WAR NO MORE:
The Story of America's Peace Seekers

LANGSTON HUGHES: *A Biography*

ALL TIMES, ALL PEOPLES: *A World History of Slavery*

THE BLACK AMERICANS: *A History in Their Own Words*

A BOOK ABOUT NAMES

STARTING FROM HOME: *A Writer's Beginnings*

THOMAS JEFFERSON: *The Revolutionary Aristocrat*

COLUMBUS AND THE WORLD AROUND HIM

BENJAMIN FRANKLIN: *The New American*

GEORGE WASHINGTON AND THE BIRTH OF OUR NATION

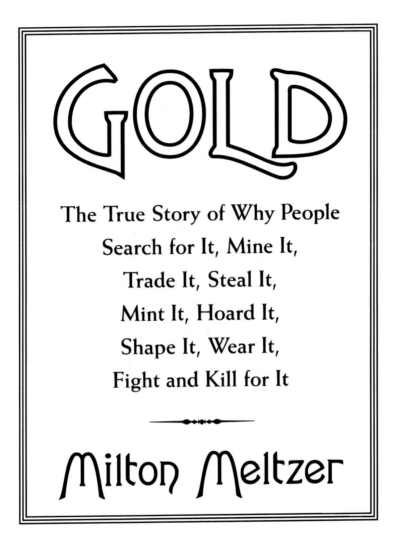

GOLD

The True Story of Why People
Search for It, Mine It,
Trade It, Steal It,
Mint It, Hoard It,
Shape It, Wear It,
Fight and Kill for It

Milton Meltzer

HarperCollins*Publishers*

Library of Congress Cataloging-in-Publication Data
Meltzer, Milton, date
    Gold : the true story of why people search for it, mine it, trade it, steal it,
mint it, hoard it, shape it, wear it, fight and kill for it / Milton Meltzer.
        p.   cm.
    Includes bibliographical references and index.
    Summary: Discusses the value of gold and how it has been sought after
and used in countries around the world throughout history.
    ISBN 0-06-022983-7. — ISBN 0-06-022984-5 (lib. bdg.)
    1. Gold—Juvenile literature. [1. Gold.] I. Title.
TN420.M5   1993   92-44497
553.4'1—dc20   CIP
                                                                       AC

Typography by Elynn Cohen
1   2   3   4   5   6   7   8   9   10
❖
First Edition

For Mary Ellen Casey,
in appreciation

A C K N O W L E D G M E N T S

Every effort has been made to locate the copyright holders of all copyrighted materials and secure the necessary permission to reproduce them. In the event of any questions arising as to their use the publisher will be glad to make changes in future printings and editions.

We gratefully acknowledge the Picture Collection of the New York Public Library as a resource for many of the illustrations in this book.

In addition we acknowledge the following individuals and institutions, the illustrations provided to us, and list the pages on which the illustrations appear:

Pages 4, 14, 18, 24, 25, 45, 46, and 110: The Granger Collection • Page 9: Photography by Egyptian Expedition, The Metropolitan Museum of Art • Page 23: E. F. Smith Memorial Collection • Pages 33, 34, 97, and 126: South Dakota Tourism Board • Pages 29, 57, 60, and 94: New York Public Library Picture Collection • Page 58: The Metropolitan Museum of Art, The Michael C. Rockefeller Memorial Collection, Bequest of Nelson A. Rockefeller, 1979 • Page 59: The Metropolitan Museum of Art, Bequest of Alice K. Bache, 1974 and 1977 • Pages 68, 72, and 73: California State Library • Page 74: American Antiquarian Society • Page 82–83: Crocker Art Museum • Page 104: New South Wales State Library • Page 113: UN Photo 155286/Allan Tannenbaum • Page 136: Weidenfeld & Nicolson Ltd./Richard Came • Page 138: The Metropolitan Museum of Art, Rogers Fund, 1962 • Page 139: The Metropolitan Museum of Art, Fletcher Fund, 1954 • Page 142: The Metropolitan Museum of Art, Munsey Fund, 1932.

❧ Contents ❧

GOLD!

❧ Introduction ❧

Once upon a time there was a kingdom whose ruler was enormously rich. Each morning after breakfast his servants covered the king's body with gold dust, and he strutted about all day, shining gloriously golden. In the evening after supper his servants placed him on a flower-decked barge that floated on the royal lake, and the king jumped into the water to wash off the gold dust. Then, to show their devotion to the king, his subjects tossed offerings of golden objects into the lake.

The king's legendary country was called El Dorado. In Spanish it means "the gilded one."

This legend probably grew out of a religious custom of the Chibcha Indians. They lived in the highlands of South

El Dorado, the legendary city on the shore of an imaginary lake. At top left a group of travelers portage their boats to the lake from a river. A line engraving of 1599.

America in the region known today as Colombia. The Chibcha anointed each new chief with resinous gums and coated his body with gold dust. The chief then plunged into the sacred Lake Guatavita and washed off the gold as an offering to the gods of the Earth.

This Chibcha ritual died out before the Spanish conquistadores came to the New World in the early 1500s. But when they arrived, the legend of El Dorado, a whole country filled with golden treasure, was still alive. The conquistadores launched a long series of expeditions to find the fabled riches of El Dorado. Their quest for "the gilded one" unearthed no trace of him or his golden land. But it had a profound effect upon the lives of the native peoples of the Americas.

Just as gold itself has powerfully influenced the ways of humankind the world over for thousands of years.

A Passion for Gold

The world has known gold for at least 5,000 years. People have searched for it, mined it, traded it, minted it into coins, shaped it into crowns and jewelry, hoarded it, displayed it, stolen it, and killed for it. In the minds of countless millions it is the true measure of wealth.

What is it?

Gold is a metal, one of the heaviest. It is twice as heavy as lead. A small piece of gold feels weighty in the hand. Yet it is soft, too. So soft that artisans can easily shape it into an immense variety of beautiful forms. An ounce of gold can be hammered into a thin sheet covering 100 square feet or drawn into a fine golden wire 50 miles long.

Gold's value depends in part on its scarcity. There isn't enough mined to satisfy the demand for it, which keeps the price high. Yet plenty of it exists in the earth—if we could only get to it. The trouble is, this precious metal is heavily concentrated in the Earth's core. If we could sink a hole into the Earth 2,000 miles deep, there would be more gold available than has been found all through time. But mining engineers thus far have been able to go only a bit over 2 miles down. Beyond that depth, the pressure of the earth above would be terribly dangerous to workers trying to extract the gold.

It's almost impossible to destroy gold. Neither corrosion nor acids that spoil other metals can harm gold. Gold treasure carried on ships wrecked in the ocean hundreds or thousands of years ago is still as good as ever; salt water does not harm it.

The yellow metal has a seemingly endless life. Gold that decorated an emperor's throne or a queen's robe in ancient times may be part of the gold ring you wear today. For gold

RIGHT: *The massive gold mask of the young Egyptian king Tutankhamen. The sculptured mask was placed over the head of the mummy.*

objects have been melted and remelted time and again and made into new objects long after. Perhaps you have read of the tomb of Tutankhamen, the boy pharaoh who died in Egypt more than 3,000 years ago. When his tomb was discovered by the archeologist Howard Carter in 1922, the gold sarcophagus and the gold ornaments inside it shone as brilliantly as on the day "King Tut" was buried.

In ancient times gold was believed to be the emblem of eternal life. Throughout history it has been a sign of wealth and power, and a driving force for adventure and discovery. The story of the hunt for the Golden Fleece by Jason and his Argonauts in Greek mythology demonstrates how old is the passion for gold. (A fleece of gold is not as strange as it seems, for fleece was used by early sluicers to trap the heavy metal in streams and rivers. Possibly the sheepskin Jason sought contained a rich coating of gold granules. Or the root of the legend may have been voyages of pirates sailing in the Black Sea to plunder the gold-mining camps along its shores.)

In the Bible, the first metal mentioned is gold. Genesis (2:11–12) says that the first river coming out of Eden is Pison, "which compasseth the whole land of Havilah, where

For the scientifically minded, gold is 19.32 times the weight of its own volume of water. Its symbol is Au, atomic number 79, atomic weight 197.2, melting point 1,945° Fahrenheit.

A karat is a unit of purity equal to one part in twenty-four. Thus, pure gold is said to be 24 karat, and 18-karat gold would be eighteen parts gold and six parts other metal; 14k is fourteen parts gold and ten parts other metal. Expressed another way, gold's quality can be rated in parts per thousand. Thus, to speak of 995 gold is to say the gold is 99.5 percent pure; 999 is the even higher quality: 99.9 percent pure, also called 99.9% fine.

NOTE: Nothing less than 10k can legally be marketed or sold as gold jewelry in the United States. Anything less is not considered real gold. Most commercial gold jewelry in the United States is 14-karat.

there is gold; And the gold of that land is good. . . ." Later, Genesis (13:2) notes that Abraham was "very rich in cattle, in silver, and in gold."

Men and women have wanted gold so badly, they have lied and cheated and murdered to get it. A king of ancient Thrace, a region of southeastern Europe, killed his brother-in-law for it. The daughter of a Roman noble accepted a bribe of gold to let the enemy into the fortress protecting Rome. The Roman general Crassus invaded the country of Parthia, in southwest Asia, in the first century B.C. solely to seize the gold in its treasury. When Crassus' soldiers were defeated, the Parthian king melted some of his gold and poured the hot liquid metal down the throat of Crassus. "You have thirsted for gold," he said; "now drink it."

How the ancient Greeks felt about gold has come down to us in a collection of ancient writings gathered by the German metal expert Georgius Agricola, in the mid-1500s A.D. Said Aristodemus, ruler of Messenia in the eighth century B.C., "Money makes the man. No one who is poor is either good or honored." (Greek money was usually in the form of gold or silver.) That cynical view is voiced too by Timocles, who said, "Money is the life and soul of mortal men. He who has not heaped up riches for himself wanders like a dead man amongst the living." And again, from the Roman poet Sextus Propertius of the first century B.C.: "The greatest rewards come from gold. By gold, love is won; by gold, faith is destroyed; by gold, justice is bought."

It was in the same ancient period that the Scythian people lived around the Black Sea. Originally nomadic horsemen from western Asia, they settled in Ukraine around 600 B.C. They found gold in the rivers and in the Ural Mountains. Their artisans created stunning objects out of gold. The Scythian goldsmiths shaped the gold into elaborate combs, cups, vases, and jewelry. When a Scythian ruler died, his wives and servants were killed, and all of them were buried in a mass grave, filled with golden objects. Many of these beautiful Scythian works of art, unearthed by archeologists, are now displayed in museums.

One of the greatest gold hunters of all time was Alexander the Great. At the age of twenty he inherited the kingdom of Macedonia in northern Greece. In 334 B.C., with an army of 40,000 soldiers, he advanced from Macedonia into Asia to conquer the Persian Empire. That done, he marched through much of western Asia, made a side trip to take over Egypt, and then went on to India. He died of a fever at thirty-three believing himself to be a god. He had conquered more lands than any general before him, and soon myriad legends about

his life arose. But one thing factual about him was his lust for gold. He took men experienced in finding gold with him, always on the lookout for rich deposits of the precious metal. Nor did he neglect the public treasuries and private pockets in his path. He looted the civic wealth wherever he marched, and forced citizens to hand over their gold coins. So much wealth poured into his money bags that it was said he not only conquered the ancient world, he owned it.

To lighten the burden of his troops on the path of conquest, Alexander often buried his golden plunder in secret places. Treasure hunters have found some of it, but much probably still remains to be unearthed.

Just as in today's world nations go to war over the control of oil fields, so in ancient times they fought over gold mines. Carthage, the ancient city-state on the northern coast of Africa near Tunis, sent its merchants, soldiers, and explorers into southern Europe and down the West African coast to build a powerful empire. One of the regions they dominated was Spain, a land rich in gold mines. Many thousands of en-

LEFT: *The Roman legions attack Carthage in 149 B.C., in the war caused partly by the desire of one power for the gold mines controlled by the other. A nineteenth-century wood engraving.*

slaved whites were worked to death extracting gold from those mines. Meanwhile Rome, poor in gold, looked jealously at Carthage's fat profits from Spain. Capture of those mines was a major reason Rome fought Carthage during what are called the Punic Wars. Finally, in 146 B.C., Rome's legions conquered the mercenary troops paid for by Carthaginian gold. Spain became another Roman province, and Carthage was destroyed.

Shekels, Bezants, Florins, Ducats, and Guineas

*I*t's hard to realize that for a good part of life on Earth, there were no coins. Their use in trade is a relatively recent development. The first trading was done by barter. A hunter carried the skin of an animal he had caught to a farmer and exchanged it for some wheat. In the *Iliad*, the poet Homer tells of ships landing in Greek ports carrying casks of wine to exchange for hides or cattle or slaves.

Not an easy way to do business! But what other way was there? Each party to the trade had some idea of the amount of labor that went into his product. If it took three days to make a cooking pot, then it would be a fair swap for three knives that each took a day to make. In some rural or mountain districts isolated from the rest of the world, this barter

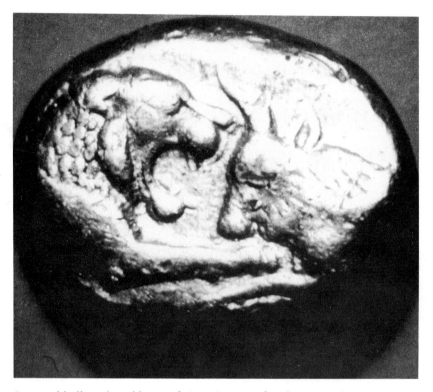

Lion and bull on the gold coin of King Croesus of Lydia, 561–540 B.C.

system has lasted into the twentieth century.

It was the rulers of ancient Lydia, a country in Asia Minor legendary for its wealth, who were the first to use coined money. The story goes that the Lydians had gotten rich by conquering King Midas of Phrygia, a neighboring country. In return for a favor, a god had granted Midas the power of turning everything he touched into gold. But Midas soon tired of his gift when even food became gold in his hand. Finally the god allowed Midas to wash away the power in a river, whose sands then turned to gold. (Again, legend is rooted in fact, for there was a real King Midas of Phrygia in the eighth century B.C.)

As Lydia grew wealthy on Phrygia's gold-bearing streams, one of its rulers around 600 B.C. ordered gold coins to be minted. These first Lydian coins were crude, more oblong than circular, with the head of a lion facing a bull on one side. They all had a uniform, standard weight.

For a long time before this, raw gold and silver had been used as the media of exchange. Chunks of these metals in all different sizes passed back and forth. Merchants had to weigh them on balances to establish their value. Later Babylon used shekels, bits of gold that looked like small pieces of yellow dough and weighed 8.34 grams each. The Hebrews too had shekels but theirs all weighed 16.4 grams each. In India the minting of gold and silver coins began about the same time as in Lydia, about six centuries before the Christian era, though rice was used as currency for a long time.

The first ruler to have his own portrait stamped on his coins was Darius the Great of Persia (about 500 B.C.). Usually the coin showed him as a hunting bowman. Traders understood that the powerful kingdom of Persia guaranteed the weight and purity of the coins, and accepted them without question.

It had taken thousands of years, but people at last had a reliable medium of exchange. It made a vast difference in how the world did business. A merchant could send a ship to a far-off country carrying only a bag of coins to exchange for a cargo of merchandise.

The first currency to reach beyond many national boundaries goes back to Alexander the Great. When the young general took Persia, he found 1,000 tons of gold and silver ingots in the treasury, and 250 tons of gold coins. He had the gold and silver bars minted into coins, handing them out generously to his favorites at court and to his troops. The coins he minted were used throughout the vast regions his power had reached, and after his death the coins continued to nourish trade everywhere.

A new gold coin was minted by the Emperor Constantine in A.D. 325, when he became ruler of the Roman Empire. Called the "bezant," the coin was used by merchants from China to Ethiopia and from Russia to the Adriatic. It contained 65 grains of gold and for nearly 800 years was the dominant world currency. (A grain is a tiny measure adopted when merchants wanted to have a uniform weight for gold coins. See the Appendix for equivalents in more familiar units.)

For several generations after the reign of Charlemagne (A.D. 800–814) in western Europe, about the only money to be minted was the silver penny. But in the 1200s Italy, France, and England began to mint coins of gold. In Italy the coins made in Florence were called florins; the coins of Venice were called ducats. They were the two most valuable moneys in Europe. The less valuable coins were made of silver, bronze, copper, or lead.

England introduced a new gold coin in the 1600s. It was called a guinea, named after the part of the Gold Coast in Africa that is now Ghana. The Company of Royal Adventurers of England trading in Africa were encouraged to bring back gold and allowed to place their stamp upon the coins minted from it. The image was an elephant with a castle perched on its broad back.

In Japan, a money economy was established in the 1600s A.D. But the circulation of gold, silver and copper coins didn't reach down to most of the people for a long time. Rice—the old money—hung on. A load of rice was swapped for a load of herrings.

Of course, counterfeiters came along quickly to mint fake

The ancient art of alchemy refers to the changing of one element into something else—a transformation. Where interest in alchemy first arose no one is sure. Perhaps Egypt? China? And then moved westward? It centered chiefly around experiments with metals and chemical materials. The driving purpose was to transform inferior metals into gold, considered to be the most perfect of metals and therefore the most valuable.

It was once imagined that there must be a substance—called the philosopher's stone or an elixir—that could change metals into gold and even restore youth to a man. What the alchemists tried to do with their apparatus was tinged with magic. Like the Good Fairy, the successful alchemist would find the philosopher's stone, acquire great wealth, and divine the meaning of life. It was in this searching that the science of chemistry had its beginnings. The experiments of alchemists never transformed lead into gold, but they did point to useful discoveries.

———◆◆◆———

The magic art of alchemy was often portrayed in symbols. Here in the alchemical production of gold, the gray wolf in the foreground (antimony sulfide) devours the king (gold alloy) lying on the ground, after which it is burned on a pyre (background), consuming the wolf and restoring the king to life (pure gold).

coins. They learned to do it so accurately, experts sometimes failed to detect it. Master craftsmen in a crooked trade, they could fake all kinds of coins, from ancient to modern. A German forger of the 1800s has been credited with faking over

A money changer and his wife, depicted by Quentin Metsys, a Flemish artist of the Renaissance.

A banking house in Florence in the early fifteenth-century. A fresco by Niccolo Gerini.

600 kinds of coins. So many false coins are marketed nowadays that major museums have acquired ingenious devices to detect them.

But where is the real stuff, the true gold, found?

THREE

Where It Is and How to Get at It

*I*f you were hunting for gold in the crust of the planet Earth, you'd find, on average, only a very tiny amount of gold per ton. While it is widespread in small amounts in volcanic rock, it's unusual to find masses of gold-bearing rock rich enough to be worth mining. When that happens, "GOLD RUSH!" blazes in the headlines.

Why or how such enriched veins occur is not certain. Geologists believe gold, along with other minerals, has been carried up from great depths by rising hot water. This pressurized water follows fractures or cracks formed by the earth's movements, until it meets cooler rock, usually within a few thousand feet of the surface.

When the heat and pressure lessen, the minerals start to crystallize. Gold, if present, gathers at broken surfaces and gradually fills spaces along cracks to form veins. Several minerals mix to make up a vein—quartz, copper, lead as well as gold. If the various mineral materials continue moving up, they mingle with groundwater and emerge at the surface. At the surface, weather and erosion soon begin to disintegrate the rocks and minerals. They break up into boulders, gravel, sand, flakes, and finer particles, and are washed into gullies, creeks, and rivers.

Most commonly grains of gold in rocks can't be seen. Sometimes flakes of gold big enough to be visible occur. And less often the gold appears in masses or veins.

Gold can also be found in seawater—and in astonishing quantities. The hitch is, it takes so much energy to recover it that the process isn't profitable.

How is gold obtained? The two main methods are placer mining (also called panning) and vein mining. When the metal is found in scattered deposits of sand and gravel in rivers or streams—alluvial deposits—placer mining is used to separate out the gold.

Most individual placer miners today still use a simple old

device—the pan, a circular dish of sheet iron or tinned steel, maybe 10–16 inches in diameter—to extract the gold by washing. They fill the pan about two thirds with the "pay dirt" to be washed and hold it in the stream. They take out the bigger stones by hand, and shake and twist the gravel and sand quickly enough to let the water carry most of the lighter material over the edge, while the heavier stuff—the gold—stays on the bottom.

Soon more advanced devices were used to sort out larger quantities of gold. The cradle is a box mounted on rockers, with a perforated bottom of sheet iron on which the pay dirt is placed. When water is poured on the dirt and the cradle is rocked, the lighter stuff passes through the holes in the bottom to a canvas sheet.

For larger-scale mining, and where plenty of water is available, sluices are generally used. These are shallow troughs, about 12 feet long, 16–20 inches wide, and 1 foot deep. The troughs are often joined in a gently sloping series, sometimes totaling several hundred feet. The U-shaped trough has crossbars firmly fastened to the rough bottom—something like a washboard. They catch the heavier particles so they won't be washed down the slope. Pay dirt is shoveled in, water is poured down, larger stones are taken out by hand, and

Miners of the mid nineteenth century extracting gold by "rocking the cradle."

the materials caught behind the bars are gleaned to recover the gold.

Other more advanced placer methods are hydraulic mining and dredging.

But the most important way of getting out gold is vein or

lode mining. There is so much gold deposited in underground rock veins that more than half the world's total gold production is from vein mining. The gold in these veins may occur in microscopic particles, in nuggets, in sheets, or in gold compounds. But no matter how nature has deposited it, the ore is costly to extract and refine. For just 1 measure of gold, miners process on the average 100,000 measures of ore.

Another source of gold is the byproducts of the mining of copper, zinc, and lead. When these baser (less valuable) metals are refined, enough gold is present in the sludge to make its recovery worthwhile. In fact, one third of all gold is produced this way.

To mine gold found underground, one basically sinks a vertical shaft down into the earth until the "reef" or vein of gold is reached. The shaft provides the means for raising and lowering the workers, tools, and equipment, and for bringing up the ore. Horizontal tunnels are then driven from the bottom of the shaft to the working face of the mine where the gold-bearing ore is found.

Of course gold ore has its limits; there's just so much of it in a mine, and sooner or later all mines will peter out. But modern technology keeps adding new devices to extend a mine's possibilities. In the early 1900s a mine going down 4,000 feet was considered a deep mine. Now a mine in South Africa has plunged 12,000 feet—or over 2.25 miles deep. Once miners used chisellike pieces of steel struck by hammers or sledges to bore holes into rock. Today, air jackhammers do the job.

Let's take a look at what it's like to sink deep into the Earth to where gold is mined. Dressed in boots, an oil slicker, and a hardhat with a battery-powered lantern fixed to the crown, you enter a steel cage at the surface. Squealing and groaning, it drops faster and faster into the surrounding darkness. Only a dim light glows overhead in the cage. The lights of side tunnels flash by as your ears pop, and moisture drops onto your helmet, running down the front of your slicker. There is a rush and a hollow rumble, as if the sound of your descent were plunging to the bottom of the shaft, then echoing back up to you.

At the 3,000-foot level the cage stops at a brightly lit tunnel with a railroad track running along its floor. A water pipe snakes along the ceiling on one side. A mine train rolls down the track toward you, follows a switch, and disappears somewhere into another crosscut. The air is hot and heavy with moisture, and after you walk only a few yards along the track, sweat runs off your body.

Standing in the crosscut, you look toward the mine face. The passage to it is only 40 inches high, just high enough to allow crews to crawl forward with their jackhammers, explosives, and shovels. You wonder if claustrophobia will fill you with panic. But you crouch down on all fours and with a kind of squirming hand crawl reach a point where three miners are at work. You can see them only by the light of the hard-hat lanterns. At this depth, the pressure is over 4,000 pounds per square inch inside the rock—as compared to about 14 pounds per square inch at the surface. And the pressure increases with the depth. Sometimes, you've heard, in deeper mines, the pressure becomes so great that the rock spontaneously explodes like a bursting grenade, spraying deadly chunks in all directions. You remember reading that six miners were killed recently in one such explosion.

You watch one of the miners as he lies on his back, balancing a drill with a booted foot, the handles in his fists. A crouched assistant helps apply pressure on the tool. The noise of the air drill thunders and roars with a staccato ca-

Air jackhammer bores holes in a South Dakota mine.

dence. You glance around and wonder if the wood-and-rock pillars will really support the tremendous weight of the rock overhead.

The miners are drilling a pattern of holes along the face. The blaster packs the holes with explosives, moves off to a

Gold-bearing ore being finely ground prior to mixing with potassium cyanide.

safe place, and ignites the charges. It blows rock loose, winch scrapers gather it, and mechanical loaders lift the gold-bearing ore onto cars for transport to hoists.

Once above ground, the rock is first crushed into walnut-sized chunks, then ground in ball mills. Next the ore is mixed with potassium cyanide, which dissolves gold from the rock. Zinc shavings are added to attract the potassium cyanide from the gold. The dissolved zinc salts are washed away, the gold is returned to a solid, and is now ready to be melted and refined in electric furnaces, then poured into 1,000-ounce bars for transport to a refinery.

Mining wasn't always like this. Let's see what it was like thousands of years ago.

FOUR

Slaves and Ants: Miners of the Ancient World

*I*n the ancient world quantities of gold were found in places with such names as Ophir, Sheba, Uphaz, and Parvain, as well as in today's more familiar places such as Arabia, India, and Spain. By the time of Christ—2,000 years ago—gold seekers had also unearthed deposits in Thrace (Greece), Italy, and Anatolia (in Turkey).

But the oldest site of gold mining, its cradle, was in ancient Egypt. The ancient western world learned from Egypt how to mine gold and to extract the metal from the ore, refine it, and prepare it for use. The Egyptians circulated gold in rings of fixed weight as a form of money.

Earlier we mentioned the golden treasures found in the

tomb of Tutankhamen. That gold came from the granite hills on both sides of the Red Sea. One of the Red Sea mines, in the hills of Sudan, is among the world's oldest. Since gold was discovered there about 1500 B.C., the mine has been worked at various times.

The Roman Empire drew the minerals it needed from many widely scattered mines. Its gold came from Romania, France, and Spain. The search for minerals was a major force in the Roman Empire's drive for conquest. Emperor Vespasian (ruled A.D. 69–79) drew the equivalent of tens of millions of dollars a year from the gold of Spain alone.

As the Spanish mines began to play out, the Romans exploited the mines of their Balkan provinces. But when Emperor Trajan (ruled A.D. 98–117) conquered the gold-producing land of Dacia (Romania), most of the native miners were killed during the fighting. So the emperor brought in a tribe of experienced miners from Albania.

It was slaves who worked those ancient mines. The Greek historian Diodorus Siculus describes their conditions in the mines of Egypt during the first century B.C.:

There they throng, all in chains, all kept at work continuously day and night. There is no relaxation, no means of escape; for, since they speak a variety of languages, their guards cannot be corrupted by friendly conversations or actual acts of kindness. Where the gold-bearing rock is very hard, it is first burned with fire, and, when it has softened sufficiently to yield to their efforts, thousands upon thousands of these unfortunate wretches are set to work on it with iron stone-cutters under the direction of the craftsman who examines the stone and instructs them where to begin. The strongest of those assigned to this luckless labor hew the marble with iron picks. There is no skill in it, only force. The shafts are not cut in a straight line but follow the veins of the shining stone. Where the daylight is shut out by the twists and turns of the quarry, they wear lamps tied to their foreheads, and there, contorting their bodies to the contours of the rock, they throw their quarried fragments to the ground, toiling on and on without intermission under the pitiless overseer's lash.

Young children descend the shafts into the bowels of the earth, laboriously gathering the stones as they are thrown down, and carrying them into the open air by the shafthead, where they are taken from them by men over thirty years, each receiving a prescribed amount, which they break on stone mortars with iron pestles into pieces as small as a vetch [a plant]. Then they are handed on to women and older men, who lay them on rows of grindstones, and standing in groups of two and three they pound them to powder as fine as the best wheaten flour.

No one could look on the squalor of these wretches, with not even a rag to cover their loins, without feeling compassion for their plight. They may be sick, or maimed, or aged, or weakly women, but there is no indulgence, no respite. All alike are kept at their labor by the lash, until, overcome by hardships, they die in their torments. Their misery is so great that they dread what is to come even more than the present, the punishments are so severe, and death is welcomed as a thing more desirable than life.

And the Roman poet Lucretius, a contemporary of Diodorus, comments on what the mines did to the men who worked them:

See you not, when men are following up the veins of silver and gold and searching with the pick quite into the bowels of the earth, what stenches exhale from below? Then what mischief do gold mines exhale! To what a state do they reduce men's faces and what a complexion they produce! Know you not by sight or hearsay how they commonly perish in a short time and how all vital power fails those to whom the hard compulsion of necessity confines in such an employment.

Such sympathetic reports of slave labor are rare. Few paid attention to the sufferings of the millions at the bottom of society.

The peoples of the Middle East had been searching for gold some 3,000 years before the Christian era began, and field archeologists have unearthed many objects and documents that indicate how gold was found and used. The miners of the ancient world often gathered gold fairly easily from certain pockets in riverbeds. These deposits were formed in prehistoric times. As streams cut through gold-bearing rock, they loosened the heavy mineral and carried it down to pools, where it settled as sand. The fifth-century

Many rulers who could find no gold in their own regions tried to acquire it by trade or conquest. The so-called "beaker people," in the third millennium B.C., roamed through western Europe. They found gold in Ireland. The Minoans on the island of Crete got gold from Asia Minor. The Scythians and the Persians took some of their gold from the Ural Mountains and even from the Altai Mountains in Siberia.

Greek historian Herodotus reported how, in India, huge ants (as big as foxes!) erected sandhills filled with gold nuggets they kicked from their tunnels. When the ferocious ants were asleep, the Indians would raid the anthills to gather the gold. Sounds like fantasy, doesn't it? But modern gold hunters have been led to rich veins of gold by finding samples of the riches beneath anthills and animal burrows.

African Empires Built on Gold

*L*ong before the Roman Empire crumbled, the people of Africa were mining gold, trading it, and making beautiful objects out of it.

Trading across the Sahara, a vast desert of stone and sand, was carried on by the Arabs using camels. What the Arabs wanted most from West Africa was its gold, though they wanted slaves and ivory too. The gold of West Africa was placer mined by the people of a forest region known as Wangara, near the Republic of Burkina Faso. In return for gold, the Arabs offered salt, copper, beads, cotton goods, and, later, guns and ammunition.

In between this gold-producing region and the Arabs lived the savanna people. They became the middlemen, the go-betweens in the trade between the other two groups. They would carry what they bought from the Arabs to the miners in the south, exchange the items for gold, and then take the gold to the Arabs. Because the savanna people controlled the gold trade, they became rich—so rich that other people tried to raid or conquer them. In self-defense the savanna people built up armies that in time overran weaker neighboring peoples. Their kings became emperors, ruling over great regions. The first to rise was the ancient empire of Ghana, and soon after that the Mali and then the Songhai empires.

About a thousand years ago an Arab trader visited the court of one of Ghana's kings. Ghana was already being called "the land of gold." It was said that one of its kings hitched his horse to a 30-pound gold nugget. The Arab wrote that the king had 200,000 warriors. His court was guarded both by huge dogs wearing gold and silver collars and by soldiers carrying shields and swords with golden handles. The king and his courtiers wore beautiful clothes ornamented with fine jewels. To support such luxury, the king taxed traders on all the goods they brought in or carried out, and the men who operated the gold mines paid an especially big tax.

Ghana's near monopoly of gold gave it a very strong trading position. West African gold was wanted in Europe as well as in North Africa and the Middle East. In earlier times the Europeans got the gold they needed—for money, ornaments, or the display of personal wealth—from mines in Europe or in Western Asia. But these sources were drying up just at the time the Ghana empire rose. So the gold used in Europe for many centuries came mostly from West Africa.

The Ghana empire began to crumble in the eleventh century, under attack by Muslim Berbers from northern Africa. Nearby, the new kingdom of Mali grew to be one of the largest empires in the world by the late 1200s. Its greatest ruler was Mānsa Mūsā, a Muslim who made Islam the official religion of the empire. (Ghana was not a Muslim kingdom.) From his capital at Timbuktu (or Tombouctou) he made a famous pilgrimage to Mecca in A.D. 1324. He took with him about 60,000 of his people. In their vanguard 500 slaves marched, each carrying a staff of gold. Eighty camels were loaded with twelve more tons of gold. As he moved through Egypt, Mānsa spent or gave away so much gold that it nearly wrecked Egypt's economy.

Ancient Mali was the richest kingdom Africa had ever known. But over the years its trade dropped off as the gold mines of Wangara began to run out. Newer mines were

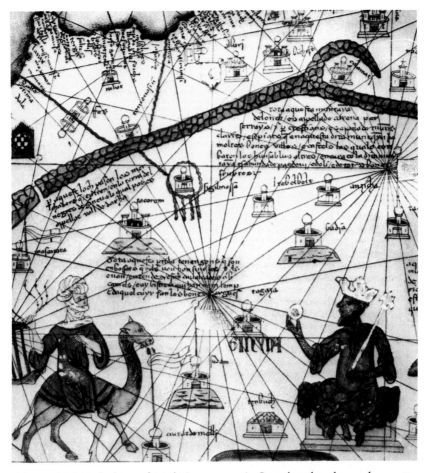

Mānsa Mūsā, the king of Mali (1312–1337). Seated on his throne, he awaits a merchant riding a camel. A detail from the Catalan atlas of 1375.

opened east of Mali, and trade routes followed. By the late 1300s Mali was weak. Control of the gold trade passed to others.

The eastern part of Africa became known to sea travelers

A camel caravan crossing the African desert. Detail from the Catalan atlas of 1375.

from Europe, the Arab world, and Asia before the tenth century A.D. Ships from far-off places traded for gold and ivory in the ports of East Africa. The gold for this trade came from an inland region called Zimbabwe, then unknown to Europeans and Arabs. As many as 7,000 ancient mine workings,

When Africans and Europeans first met to do business, there was mutual respect. Rules for the gold trade were firmly set. The African merchants made careful use of weights and measures and demanded equality in bargaining. They would bring all trading to a halt if they felt a European was trying to cheat or rob them. But as trading in slaves became a big part of this international business, the old habits of equality and mutual respect disappeared. The Europeans, ignorant of African culture and their great empires, looked with contempt on the providers of slaves and called them an inferior people. The Africans in turn said the whites never did anything except for their own profit and to the harm of the blacks.

mainly for gold, have been found there. Some were opened before A.D. 1000, and many more before 1500.

The African miners knew how to find gold-bearing rock, sometimes digging to a depth of 100 feet. They crushed the rock by hand methods and smelted it in simple blast furnaces made of anthill earth. Then they poured the gold into little molds of clay to shape it into ingots. They used the gold ingots to make ornaments for local use or to sell to coastal merchants. Most of their gold exports went to India, but some went to Indonesia and China too. In exchange the mining chiefs got Indian cotton, brass, and beads, as well as pottery and Chinese porcelain.

Although the mining technology of East and Central Africa was primitive, its master craftsmen learned to work gold into fine ornaments. How artistic these craftsmen were was discovered when archeologists digging in southern Africa uncovered the graves of chiefs along the Limpopo River. They were surprised to come upon beautifully refined gold ornaments. Some were small rhinoceros figures made of gold plate beaten to .004 inch. This was a remarkable achievement for people who worked without modern tools.

What about the gold of Europe? By the Middle Ages very little was produced there. The mines of the prehistoric period and Roman days—in Spain, Ireland, and other places—had been exhausted. "A vein of gold," someone has pointed out, "is not like a field that produces a new crop each year; it is like a bag from which one takes the contents until it is empty." Yet Europe had a money system based on gold. The shortage of the precious metal became a great nuisance. The lack of it was no doubt one of the major reasons the European powers sought to dominate and exploit the world.

The only place in Europe you could see great masses of gold in the early medieval period was Scandinavia. With incredible energy and daring the Viking ships ranged from Iceland to the borders of Turkey, from Constantinople to the Arctic Circle. Yet much of their effort was wasted in plundering. They did not bother to trade until they failed to conquer. "They preferred bloodstained, glorious gold," wrote one historian, "to a steady mercantile profit." But some of the metal they came by honestly: in wages paid to Swedish mercenaries hired by other rulers or in the price of merchandise brought down the long Russian rivers to the Baltic. Gold gleamed from the prows of their ships, and it still gleams in the showcases of Stockholm's and Copenhagen's museums.

Discovery: Golden Age and Brutal Age

Modern times are often said to date from the beginning of the Age of Discovery, in the fifteenth century. A philosopher of that time called it "undoubtedly a golden age." He was thinking of the great artists and writers and scholars who lived and worked in his day. But the more literal meaning of "golden" applies too. For kings and merchants and explorers were fired by the desire to discover new lands with rich gold deposits.

All Europe needed gold to enlarge its trade with the Far East. It was the best and most portable product to exchange for the spices, silks, and other products of the Orient. The hunt for gold, as well as for trade routes, pushed explorers into unknown seas and unknown lands.

The adventurous Portuguese and Spaniards were the first Europeans to launch great voyages of discovery. Prince Henry the Navigator of Portugal led the way. Strange that he was first, for in the 1400s his Portugal was a tiny country, a poor country with scarcely a million people. It never had enough sailors for its oceangoing ships, nor did it have enough timber to build those ships. It had to import timber and man her ships with other Europeans, with Asians, and with African slaves.

Despite all this, in 1425 Prince Henry planned and carried out the Portuguese seizure of Ceuta, a town on the North African coast opposite Gibraltar. It was one of the main terminal points in the gold trade across the Sahara. Ceuta put Portugal in a position to monopolize the import to Europe of gold, slaves, spices, and ivory.

Later, in 1481, the Portuguese built their first fort at a place they called Elmina, "the mine." It was located on a section of the coast of the Gulf of Guinea that became known as the Gold Coast because it was an important source of the metal. (It is near Cape Coast, now part of the Republic of Ghana.) This time the Portuguese did this not by conquest but by an agreement with the region's native chief. In return for other products his people delivered to Elmina large quantities of African gold for many years. But for centuries afterward neither the Portuguese nor any other European power gained access to the gold mines of the interior—not until the British fought their way into Ashanti territory in the nineteenth century.

Profits from the gold trade were immense—for the Europeans. A voyage of the 1550s showed a return amounting to about ten times the capital invested. No wonder people like Elizabeth I of England were tempted. The queen put royal money into the trade on the African coast and reaped a huge profit.

As we have seen, a trade in slaves between Africa and Europe went on at the same time as the trade in gold. Up to the time of the Atlantic voyages of Christopher Columbus and others, the slave trade had delivered in Europe some tens of thousands of slaves over centuries. But then the planting of large crops such as sugar, tobacco, rice, cotton in Brazil, the Caribbean, and the North American south created a much greater demand for slave labor. From that point until late in the 1800s—a period of some 400 years—millions upon mil-

---

Not content with honest investment, Queen Elizabeth I supported piracy on the high seas if it would add gold to the royal treasury. Sir Francis Drake had her blessing when he raided Spanish ships and stole their golden cargoes. Early in his briny career he commanded a slave-trading expedition. Then, as captain of the famous vessel the Golden Hind, he plundered Spanish settlements on the coast of South America. When he returned to England, his ship laden with gold treasure, Elizabeth knighted him. Long after, a British economist said wryly that Drake's piracy "may fairly be considered the fountain and origin of British foreign investment."

---

lions of African captives suffered transport in the ships of almost every European nation as well as the United States.

Which brings us to Columbus. He plays a key role in the stories of both gold and slavery. Often portrayed as a hero, he was no more immune to greed than the other seafaring adventurers. He piously declared that his mission was to extend Catholicism by converting the heathen to "our Holy

Faith." But he gave most of his energy to an unrelenting search for gold. "Whoever possesses gold," he said, "obtains what he will in this world."

As soon as he landed on a Caribbean island, that October 12 of 1492, Columbus asked the people if they had gold. And finding none at this first stop, he sailed on "to seek the gold and precious jewels elsewhere," he wrote. He noted in his journal that the native people "became so much our friends that it was a marvel." Their generous ways puzzled him: "Anything they have, if it be asked for, they never say no, but rather invite the person to accept it, and show as much lovingness as though they would give their hearts." But his next thought was how to enslave them, for they were "very unskilled in arms. With 50 men they could all be subjected and made to do all that I wished."

These gentle, hospitable people were rewarded with almost incredible cruelty by the Spaniards. In those first years of invasion men, women, and children were slaughtered, whole villages wiped out, land and liberty taken away, homes destroyed, women raped, thousands enslaved.

To control the rebelling Indians, Columbus built forts on Hispaniola. Using them as bases, he forced the Indians to pay him tribute in gold. He still believed that in the interior of the island, there were rich goldfields that the Indians were concealing from him. So he ordered all Indians from the age of fourteen up to collect a fixed amount of gold every three months. Each person who delivered the tribute of gold was given a copper token to hang around the neck. Indians found without that token had their hands cut off and were left to bleed to death.

Columbus had set the Indians an impossible task, for what little gold Hispaniola contained was mostly dust, found in the beds of its mountain streams. The Admiral coveted gold ornaments worn by the Indians that had been made one by one, over the years, of gold dust gathered by many generations of Indians. (By now the Spaniards had robbed the Indians of all those ornaments.)

In 1513 gold was discovered in Cuba, and the Spaniards rushed over from Hispaniola. But it turned out that Cuba had even less gold than Hispaniola. Not until the Spanish invaders conquered Mexico, Peru, and Colombia later in the 1500s did they believe they had at last struck it rich. It was 1532 when Francisco Pizarro entered the empire of the Inca in Peru. He came with 200 foot soldiers and 100 horsemen.

Atahualpa, the Sun King, had an army of at least 30,000 men. Climbing up to the Inca city of Cajamarca, Pizarro made gestures of friendship. The unsuspecting ruler entertained the Spaniards with dancing girls and the music of pipes and drums. Suddenly Pizarro signaled his men to fire a cannon. At the terrifying boom, his men shot their muskets point-blank at the stunned Inca warriors. Two thousand Indian soldiers, panicked by these strange white men who could hurl lightning through their sticks, fell dead as the Spaniards fired round after round. Only one Spaniard was wounded.

Atahualpa was taken prisoner. You can regain your freedom, Pizarro told him, if you give me a roomful of gold. The Sun King sent messengers throughout the land to bring gold to the city. Porters and llamas flocked in, carrying vases, bowls, religious figures, ornaments—all of gold. It must have been a museum curator's dream of the goldsmith's art gathered under one roof. But Pizarro, an illiterate peasant, saw only gleaming gold, not beautiful craftsmanship. He ordered Incan workers to build clay furnaces and melt down the gold into bars he could carry back home. More than six tons of gold artifacts—the fruit of centuries of Inca culture—were destroyed.

PIZZARO.

Francisco Pizarro, the Spanish conqueror of Peru.

A bargain had been made—a man's life for a roomful of gold. The Inca ruler had kept his part, but not the treacherous Pizarro. He strangled Atahualpa in a public execution. Some ten years later greed and ambition did Pizarro in. A band of his enemies surprised him at dinner and murdered him.

Those brilliant ornaments and temple decorations that dazzled Pizarro were deceptive. Like the gold of Hispaniola, they were the products of long and careful hoarding. Most of

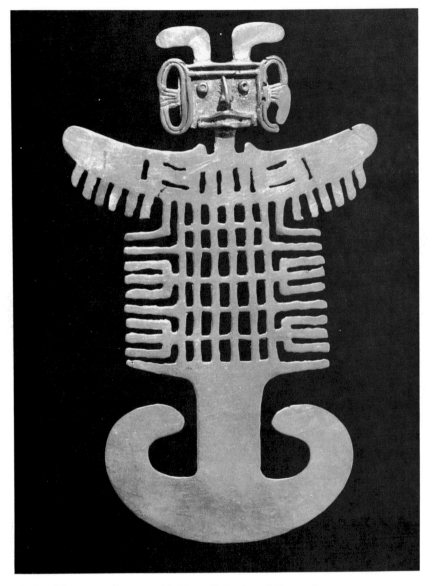

Stylized figure pendant in gold. From Colombia, fifth–tenth centuries.

A gold funerary mask, with painted overlays. From Peru, twelfth–fourteenth centuries.

the gold had been gathered from small deposits in the streams, not taken out of gold-rich mines. Uncounted years had gone into the accumulation of that gold. The hoards were not really enormous.

Theodore de Bry, a Flemish engraver, illustrated voyages and travels of the sixteenth century. This print shows Native Americans digging in the sands of a river in search of gold.

At first the Spaniards were content to look for kings to plunder or graves to loot. Then they turned to the hunt for mines. Not gold, however, but unbelievably rich deposits of silver were discovered. The greatest, found in 1545 at Potosí in Bolivia, started a tremendous silver rush. Spaniards with their Indian slaves flooded in, and within eighteen months the barren, mountainous region contained 14,000 people. By the end of the century a large mining industry was sending huge amounts of silver annually to Spain.

On a much smaller scale, gold was discovered and mined in Chile, and in the upper regions of South America the Spanish called New Granada. The richest gold deposits, however, were found in 1695, not by the Spanish, but by the Portuguese, in Brazil, in the eastern region now known as Minas Gerais.

Adventurers poured in from all over Portugal's empire, joined by other gold-hungry foreigners. A new era began in colonial Brazil. Young and old, rich and poor, noble and peasant, layman and clergy came to the mines, driven by a gold fever that would not be equaled for over 150 years, until the California gold rush of 1849.

Many of the miners were whites without enough capital to be effective. But others, more fortunate, supervised the labor of black slaves bought on long-term credit. The majority of these miners had five or six slaves; the richest owned between thirty and fifty.

A boom in the slave trade between Brazil and Africa began. Work in the goldfields was brutal, and the slaves' lives were short. One missionary said, "Their labor is so hard and their sustenance so small, they are reckoned to live long if they hold out seven years." By 1735 there were about 145,000 African slaves in Brazil's gold-mining areas.

The mining techniques, whether placer or deep shaft, were brought from West Africa, for the Portuguese operators knew less about mining than their slaves. And whether they worked along the rivers or in underground tunnels, the slave miners labored hard and long and were treated, housed, clothed, and fed badly. They were often forced to eat and sleep where they worked. "Since when they work they are bathed in sweat," wrote one observer, "with their feet always in the cold earth, on stones, or in water, their pores close and they become so chilled that they are susceptible to many dangerous illnesses. . . . Dead slaves were buried in heaps daily." And like miners everywhere, they often suffered death or mutilation from accidents. Able to endure their burdens only when fortified by brandy, many became alcoholics.

With the new supply of gold from Europe's colonies in the Americas, the world stock of gold increased steadily. Some of the precious metal flowed to the Far East to pay for silk, pepper, spices, drugs and pearls and more and more gold coins were minted by the European powers. But kings and nobles also hoarded gold, passing on to their heirs chests chockful of gold coins and gold ornaments. Hoarding didn't help the economy, for it kept the gold out of circulation. "Unemployed currency," it's called.

SEVEN

Gold Rush!

What happened in Brazil in 1695 was the nearest thing to a gold rush the world had yet seen. But that free movement of large numbers of people to where gold had been discovered didn't last long. The Portuguese king saw to that. He clamped down by taking direct control of gold mining in the colony. No longer was it free people out to better themselves who did the mining. It was slaves being exploited to better the king.

Something like that happened on the edge of Siberia, too. Russian gold mining began in 1744, when gold was rediscovered by chance in the Ural Mountains. The czar, like the Portuguese king, quickly took the mines over and forced serfs (peasants bound to the soil) to do the hard labor. Now and then private businessmen were encouraged to discover and develop new mines, but little came of it. Then in the early 1800s alluvial deposits were found, some worked by the Russian crown, some by private owners on whose land gold was found.

The mining was mostly done by serfs and convicted criminals. Forced to labor without reward, they sometimes stole gold and smuggled it out for sale. One mine operator, an Englishman brought in by the czar, used to keep the gold in an iron box in his house in the forest. He was murdered for it. The German scientist Alexander von Humboldt, who traveled throughout Russia and Brazil in the 1800s, reported that neither the Russian serfs nor the Brazilian slaves developed any real skills in mining. And why should they? What was in it for them? Nevertheless, the Russians became the foremost producers of gold until the California and Australian gold rushes.

The first genuine gold rush in American history began in Georgia. In 1828 a slave found gold in a river in northern Georgia, and another black man spotted gold in a creek near Dahlonega. Then a white named Benjamin Park picked up a stone whose deep, rich yellow color had caught his eye. And knew he had found gold.

All these discoveries were made on Cherokee land. (Perhaps the Native Americans knew there was gold there but were not eager to tell the world.) By the end of the year a gold rush was under way. Thousands of prospectors poured into Cherokee territory with picks, pans, axes, and rifles, destroying Indian property as they staked out claims. The United States government had long tried to remove Native Americans from Georgia so white settlers could take over their good farmland. The Indians had refused to go, however, believing that treaties protected them.

Andrew Jackson was now in the White House. He said the Indians didn't own the gold-rich land just because they had "seen it from the mountain or passed it in the chase." No, the gold was white America's. So the whites grabbed the Cherokee land—and made millions out of it.

The early prospectors in Georgia did placer mining, a method that called for very little investment. But as it became clear that Georgia gold was some of the purest in the world (averaging 95 percent fine), companies formed to invest in vein mining. The equipment for this kind of mining cost a lot more than most miners could afford.

Gold itself, not in the form of coins, became a direct medium of exchange in Georgia. Miners carried gold dust in small packets or even loose in their vest pockets. They sold their gold to merchants, traded it for goods, or spent it on liquor in the taverns that sprang up. A large amount was sold to the federal mint in Philadelphia.

It was mostly whites who worked the mines. In off season farmers headed for the mines too. But many rich planters bought or leased goldfields and had their slaves do the work.

Mining continued in Georgia through the 1830s and 1840s, until news that gold had been discovered in California exploded. That year of 1848 saw much of the world go crazy over the prospect of finding gold. For the next eighty years people from many nations would join mass migrations in search of easy wealth. They rushed to California, to Australia, to New Zealand, to Alaska, to British Columbia, to Nevada, to Colorado, to South Africa. Many prospectors, whether successful or not, crossed oceans and continents to take part in rush after rush.

What fevered the mind was the belief that with luck and hard work, you could become a millionaire. The news of the

accidental discovery of gold in a California stream was thrillingly dramatic. If there was gold at Sutter's Mill, surely there was lots more of it nearby to be had for the digging?

Strangely, the California discovery was no discovery at all. For many years gold had been known to exist in California. Yet no one had done anything about it. As early as 1816 a mineral expert in Scotland reported there was lots of gold in California. In 1842 a Californian announced there was gold in his area and that 2,000 ounces had been extracted by placer mining. In 1846 the U.S. consul at Monterey (remember: California was still Mexican territory) reported people could earn several dollars a day by washing gold out of the sand in a plate. But, he added, "few have the patience to work for it."

Then why was so little attention paid to these first reports? One reason might be that Americans were already dreaming of expanding the nation's boundaries west to the Pacific. It might take a war with Mexico to do it, but then the gold regions would become U.S. property. As for the Mexican government, it was not anxious to attract a horde of

LEFT: *A woman brings lunch to a team using a long tom, an outgrowth of the cradle.*

miners into California. Mexican landlords in California didn't want farm workers to desert the fields for gold prospecting. And the Franciscan friars feared an influx of Americans would interfere with their attempts to convert the Indians.

Guesswork? Yes, but it suggests that many factors may shape the outcome of events. At any rate, along came a New Jersey carpenter, James Marshall, who was building a sawmill for John Sutter, his employer, on a branch of the American River, about forty miles from Sacramento. Marshall spotted some bits of yellow mineral beneath the water on January 24, 1848. Could it be gold? If it was, it would be soft and malleable. With his hammer he found he could flatten yellow chips. "By God," he said to the men working with him, "I believe I have found a gold mine!"

Using instructions he found in an old encyclopedia, Sutter tested the samples Marshall brought him. They assayed as 22-karat gold. But it was not good news for Sutter. He was wealthy enough already. A native of Switzerland, he had become a Mexican citizen in 1840 and received from the Mexican government a huge land grant of 50,000 acres. On the bank of the American River he had erected an adobe-walled

fort overlooking the agricultural empire he was building
with the help of 450 Indians he employed as servants and
farm and ranch hands. He feared if word of the gold strike
got out, he'd lose the men working for him and would be ru-
ined. But one of his men rode over to San Francisco—then a
small town—and showed some gold flakes to Isaac
Humphrey, who had mined gold in Georgia.

Humphrey got himself hired as a laborer by Sutter. Se-
cretly he built himself the same kind of rocker he had used in
the Georgia diggings. From the moment he started to wash
gravel, he obtained several ounces of gold a day. He couldn't
keep his luck quiet, and all of Sutter's men left the ranch,
stealing his cattle and horses as they went. A week later the
first news of the gold strike appeared in the *Californian*, a San
Francisco newspaper: "GOLD MINE FOUND!"

Men went crazy overnight. The *Californian* lost its staff and
was out of business within two weeks. If any greater push
was needed, it came when President Polk confirmed the discovery in his annual message to Congress in December
1848. The greatest mass migration since the Crusades
had begun. Said one observer, "The blacksmith dropped his
hammer, the carpenter his plane, the mason his trowel, the

Captain John Sutter (above) and Sutter's Mill (right), where James Marshall's discovery of gold started the California Gold Rush.

farmer his sickle, the baker his loaf. . . . All were off for the mines, some on horses, some in carts, and some on crutches, and one went in a litter." By June 1848 there was scarcely a man left in the towns of California. Soldiers deserted their posts, and so did the men sent out to capture them. Crews

jumped ship in San Francisco harbor, field hands fled the
farms, office workers abandoned their desks.

The history of California would change radically. Adven-

turers poured in from all parts of the United States and from places as distant as China and Australia. By the end of 1849 the California population had swelled by 100,000 people. The flood of "forty-niners" continued for the next two years.

Three main routes were open if you were bound for California. You could join the steady stream of wagon trains rolling from east to west across the plains, the Rockies, the Sierra. You could sail aboard one of the hundreds of ships that left eastern ports for California sailing around Cape Horn. It was a voyage of 15,000 miles, which took five to eight months. Or you could ship down the Atlantic to Panama, cross the isthmus by dugout and mule to reach the Pacific, and then sail up to San Francisco. Aboard the crowded little ships gales, scurvy, or starvation sickened or killed thousands. Taking the land route over mountain trails, gold seekers saw the wreckage of parties that had preceded them. One migrant counted, in 15 miles, 362 abandoned wagons and the dry bones of 350 horses, 280 oxen, and 120 mules.

Some miners did get rich. Lucky ones could fill a tin cup

LEFT: *Poster promising big profits for the gold-hungry willing to join a mining and trading voyage from Boston to the California goldfields.*

The Fools of Forty-Nine

1. When gold was found in for-ty-eight, the
peo-ple said 'twas gas, And
some were fools e-nough to think the
lumps were made of brass, But

A popular ditty sung in the days of the California gold rush of 1849.

what they had been told, When they start-ed af-ter gold, That they

nev - er in this world would make a pile. 2. The pile.

When gold was found in forty-eight, the people said 'twas gas,
And some were fools enough to think the lumps were made of brass,
But they soon were satisfied and started off to mine,
They bought a ship came round the Horn in the fall of forty-nine.

CHORUS:
Then they thought of what they had been told,
When they started after gold,
That they never in this world would make a pile.

The poor, the old, the rotten scows were advertised to sail,
From New Orleans with passengers, but they must pump and bail,
The ships were crowded more than full, but some hung on behind,
And others dived off from the wharf and swam till they were blind.

CHORUS

With rusty pork and stinking beef and rotten wormy bread
With captains too that never were as high as the mainmast head,
The steerage passengers would rave and swear they'd paid their passage
They wanted something more to eat besides Bologna sausage.

CHORUS

And they begun to cross the plains with oxen, holler and 'haw';
And steamers they began to run as far as Panama,
And there for months the people stayed that started after gold,
And some returned disgusted with the lies they had been told.

CHORUS

The people died on every route, they sickened and died like sheep.
And those at sea before they were dead were launched into the deep,
And those that died crossing the Plains fared not as well as that,
For a hole was dug and they was dumped along the terrible Platte.

CHORUS

with gold every day. In eleven days a team of four men took in nearly $17,000 from a claim 3,600 square feet. But few could hang on to what they earned. Inflated prices ate up the gold. One slice of bread cost a dollar, a single potato a dollar. It was a great day for profiteers. Merchants with capital brought in ample stocks and sold everything for ten times what it cost them. The men who provided entertainment also did better than most of the miners. Gamblers and saloon keepers made huge profits from miners, who clustered in foul collections of tents and shacks—places with such names as Shinbone Creek, Humbug Hill, Tin Cup Diggings, Sixbit Gulch, Cutthroat Bar, Rough and Ready, Whiskey Flat, Greenhorn Bar, Fiddletown, Angel's Camp. In one night a miner could gamble or drink away what it had taken him weeks to accumulate.

Men gambled with their lives too. In the first five years of the Gold Rush nearly a thousand people were murdered in San Francisco alone. Murder became a way of life. Men died of slit throats, crushed skulls, gunshot wounds—if they were lucky enough not to die of cholera, typhoid, malaria, or dysentery.

Quick to turn to violence, the miners made victims of the

Chinese who had been drawn across the Pacific by the lure of riches. Many thousands headed for the goldfields. Introducing better methods of mining, they were able to extract gold that earlier adventurers had missed. Soon they were the largest single ethnic group of miners in the West. One out of every four miners was from China.

But their ingenuity and success—and the color of their skin—roused white miners to jealousy and hatred. In some places they were denied the right to mine and forced out by beatings and even murder. They were taxed so heavily that many Chinese quit mining and went to work for others. "Chinatowns" sprang up to serve their own and the white miners' needs. They started laundries and opened restaurants, boardinghouses, and general stores. The Chinese were not the only targets of prejudice. The Indians who also worked for others in the mines were cheated and driven out, and so were the Mexican miners.

Few seemed to care about law and order when fabulous amounts of gold were being mined: in 1849, about $10 million worth; in 1850, $40 million, in 1852, the year of greatest production, $80 million. As earlier in Georgia, gold became currency: a "pinch" of gold dust was worth one dollar. In the

Celebrating Sunday
in a California min-
ing camp.

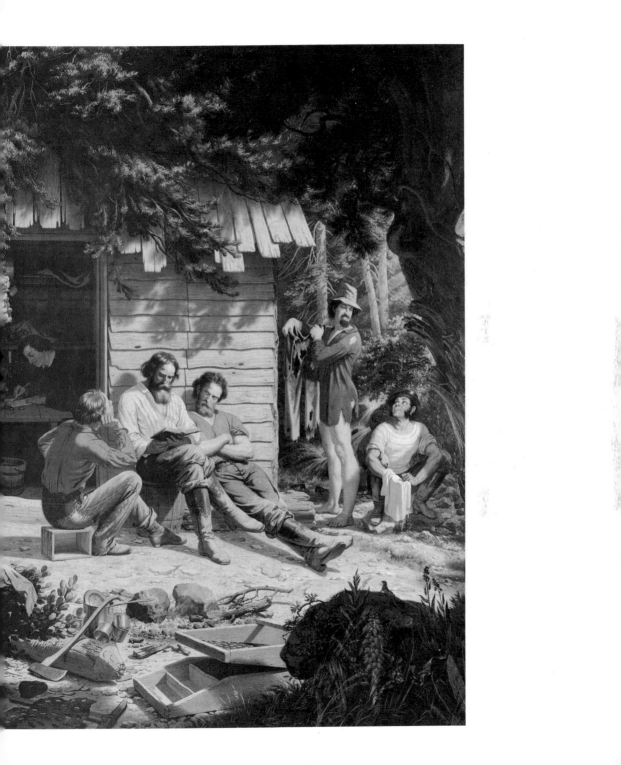

With *the onset of the gold rush, wrote the historian J. S. Holliday,*

Everything about California would change. In one astonishing year the place would be transformed from obscurity to world prominence, from an agricultural frontier that attracted 400 settlers in 1848 to a mining frontier that lured 90,000 impatient men in 1849; from a society of neighbors and families to one of strangers and transients; from an ox-cart economy based on hides and tallow to a complex economy based on gold mining; from Catholic to Protestant, from Latin to Anglo-Saxon. The impact of that new California would be profound on the nation it had so recently joined.

first year at the diggings the daily average per man was about one ounce of gold. Some took out $10, $50, $500 a day. (A lot of money when a worker might put in a ten-hour day for one dollar.)

Ironically, Polk's war with Mexico ended in Mexico's defeat scarcely one week after gold was discovered at Sutter's Mill.

Mark Twain arrived in the West soon after the gold
rush faded. He wrote this about the ghost towns he found:

You will find it hard to believe that here stood at
one time a fiercely flourishing little city, of 2,000 or
3,000 souls, with its newspaper, fire company, brass
band, volunteer militia, bank, hotels, noisy Fourth of
July processions and speeches, gambling-halls
crammed with tobacco smoke, profanity, and rough-
bearded men of all nations and colors, with tables
heaped with gold dust—streets crowded and rife
with business—town lots worth $400 a front foot—
labor, laughter, music, swearing, fighting, shooting,
stabbing—a bloody inquest and a man for breakfast
every morning—and now nothing but lifeless, homeless solitude. In no other land, in modern times, have
towns so absolutely died and disappeared, as in the
old mining regions of California.

Through the peace treaty, the United States paid Mexico
$15 million for the vast region that included the present
states of California, New Mexico, Nevada, Utah, and parts

of Colorado and Wyoming. One year after that purchase, California produced enough gold to have bought the region three times over. By 1858, California had yielded half a billion dollars in gold.

But at what a cost! For a while, in the beautiful landscape of California, men returned to a brutal level of life—ruthless, reckless, driven by an elemental greed for riches. Men shot one another in the street and the occurrence was no more noticed than a dog fight. Lynch law took over as people quickly became callous to the sight of violence. The values of common decency and caring for one another gave way to the habit of exploitation. Moneymaking became a mania.

In 1850, the year California entered the Union as a free state, three of every five inhabitants were involved in mining. But as the annual output of gold began to drop, miners drifted off, leaving ghost towns behind. Sooner or later about half the gold hunters went back to their old homes, asking themselves, Was it worth it? One wrote that it was "a living death, and a punishment of the worst kind, and the time spent here ought to be considered as a blank period in existence, and accordingly struck from the record of one's days."

Henry David Thoreau, reading in his Concord, Massachusetts, home about the gold rush, wrote: "The hog that roots his own living and so makes manure would be ashamed of such company. If I could command the wealth of all the world by lifting my finger, I would not pay such a price for it. It makes God to be a moneyed gentleman who scatters a handful of pennies in order to see mankind scramble for them. Going to California. It is only three thousand miles nearer to hell."

EIGHT

"If There Is Shooting Here, There Will Be Hanging Here"

*I*t was in 1858 that the gold craze leaped north of California. Rich goldfields had been discovered on the Fraser River in western Canada, in a colony soon to be named British Columbia. When the news reached California, the mining towns and camps emptied out. By the year's end 30,000 miners had arrived in Victoria, the jumping-off city for the diggings.

They found life in British Columbia much different from California. The landscape was threatening. The mountain snows were five feet deep, the rivers almost impossible to navigate, the canyons treacherous, the forests roadless. But miners, mechanics, and small traders rushed in, followed by cooks, fishermen, land agents, and speculators of all kinds.

They moved out from Victoria in canoes or homemade boats that swamped easily and drowned many of the passengers.

The gold was also harder to extract than in California. Found in rocks, it was fine as flour. It had to be crushed into concentrate, then cleaned with nitric acid. Mercury was used to recover the metal from the concentrate. The yield commonly was half an ounce to an ounce a day.

The colonial government, dominated by James Douglas (governor of the newly created province of British Columbia), claimed the right to all the gold deposits; no one could mine without a license costing at first 10 shillings a month and later 1 to 5 pounds a year. A tough administrator, Douglas used the military to enforce the law and gold commissioners to settle disputes.

What alarmed the Canadians was the fact that most of the miners were Americans with miserable reputations earned in California. Douglas wanted to prevent lawlessness and keep the economic benefits of the gold rush from flowing across the border. At first he tried using a police force made up entirely of runaway slaves and free blacks who had come north for the rush. But he had to give that up when whites showed only contempt for the blacks' authority.

The racism of the forty-niners that had surfaced in violence in California created the same tensions in Canada. The gold lands had belonged to the Salish Indians, who resented the white invaders. The miners plied them with liquor and enslaved the women. When many Chinese miners began to come in to do the hardest work at half the whites' pay, the racism was focused on them. A Canadian magistrate warned, "Remember, boys, if there is shooting here, there will be hanging here."

As mining inched farther north into the Fraser River Valley, richer strikes were made. Nuggets weighing a third of an ounce and some as large as six ounces were found. In one place nuggets actually littered the ground, perhaps reinforcing the perennial immigrant dream of a land whose streets were paved with gold. The surface gold was a sign to geologists that erosion had deposited it there from great veins of gold higher upstream. Big money was needed to get at those layers of gold-bearing rock. Investors came in to finance the same hydraulic methods that had devastated the California landscape.

What effect on the economy did all that new Canadian gold have? It fed into the world's money supply, pumping up a speculative fever. People relied more and more on credit to do business. When they couldn't pay their debts, a collapse was inevitable. Then in 1857 an insurance company in Ohio failed. It touched off the worst financial panic in twenty years. Banks closed, businesses shut their doors, trade was crippled.

But still another gold rush was just around the corner. A band of prospectors from Georgia made their way into a corner of Colorado. They were drawn by stories told by Indians of gold somewhere in the Rockies. It was a wild region dominated by Pike's Peak. When the rumors of gold were confirmed in 1859, a rush started. "Pike's Peak or Bust" was the slogan. By midyear some 10,000 people had flooded in, establishing a large town to be called Central City. Those miners who found sites where simple placer mining could be done stayed on. The others soon left, however. Corporations came in with the money to hire men to sink the deep shafts needed to reach most of the gold.

Rumors of gold in the Black Hills of Dakota began to circulate just before the Civil War began. But the war and an uprising of Sioux Indians in the territory kept gold seekers away. Then in 1868 the United States signed a treaty with the Sioux creating an enormous reservation that included all of what is now South Dakota west of the Missouri River. It made the spectacular Black Hills with all its mineral wealth the exclusive property of the Indians—forever. The federal government guaranteed the Sioux that no whites could enter or take away any of their territory.

Long experience showed that treaties with Indians meant little to whites. All this one did was to postpone a gold rush for a while—until hard times hit America in 1873; then it was 1857 all over again: a furious pace of growth was powered by a rage for speculation. When a big bank collapsed, down went hundreds of other banks and businesses. Panic spread swiftly as millions lost their jobs. They marched in the streets demanding "bread for the needy, clothes for the naked, houses for the homeless." Desperation drove many to seek a way out of poverty in the goldfields.

Was there really gold in the Black Hills? President Grant sent General George Armstrong Custer to find out. Always bent on grand display, Custer took along a dozen infantry companies, cavalry, artillery, Indian scouts, and two gold miners. One of them found gold in the high ridge that rose 4,000 feet and ranged 110 miles long and 40 miles wide. The news fired the hopes of men who needed to make a living somehow, somewhere. As they began to move toward Indian territory, the army issued an order barring all trespassers.

But the miners slipped through the army lines to reach the

place where Custer had found gold. One jump ahead of the Indians, the army kicked the miners out. More came, more were sent back, still more came. Trouble ahead: The land belonged to the Sioux. The miners were trespassing. Would the government keep its promise to protect Indian rights?

President Grant tried to get the Indians to sell their land. When they refused, the government called off the army. The miners rushed into the Black Hills. The president blamed his withdrawal of the troops on the greed of whites—both the miners and the soldiers. If he had continued to use troops to remove the miners, he told Congress, the soldiers would have deserted to prospect for gold themselves.

The result of the government's failure to keep its word was war with the Sioux. It led to the massacre of Custer and his men in the Battle of Little Big Horn in June 1876. But it was only a temporary victory for the Indians. In October the soldiers defeated Chiefs Sitting Bull and Crazy Horse, ending the war.

But not the restless hunt for gold. Now miners poured into the Black Hills. They found gold in streams everywhere. Most of the men were loners, without capital or know-how. But placer mining didn't require that. Still, it took vast amounts of labor to get gold out of the streams, and there was

no guarantee of decent returns. Men were lucky if they made a day's wages. But if a few struck it rich, it lured others in.

Real wealth came only when great lodes of gold were discovered farther north in the Hills. That happened at a place called Deadwood Gulch. By the summer of 1876 it was a roaring gold camp of 25,000 people. The greatest strike was made by prospectors working their way up above Deadwood Gulch. The lode was called the Homestake. It proved to be the richest of all the mines in the Western Hemisphere.

Developing it took capital on a grand scale, for treatment of the ore required extensive use of machinery and chemicals. The Homestake mining was organized as a big business. Three wealthy men made up a syndicate to buy Homestake. The one who ran the company was George Hearst. The gold he got out of Homestake was the foundation of a great fortune that bought up silver and copper mines too, paid for the San Simeon cattle ranch, and financed the publishing empire run by his son, William Randolph Hearst.

That a Homestake mining operation could make money,

LEFT: *George Armstrong Custer, the self-dramatizing general, in a photo by Matthew Brady, made shortly before the young cavalryman died in battle with Indians at the Little Bighorn.*

Outlaws and lawmen made Deadwood Gulch a legend in Western history. The mining town lived by its own rules, for the federal government had no control over Indian land. The miners set up their own local government and their own courts to maintain some degree of law and order. But bloody brawls and deadly gunfights were common in the street and in the taverns and dance halls. Names that still ring romantically in books and movies and on television—Wild Bill Hickok, Buffalo Bill, Calamity Jane, Wyatt Earp, Bat Masterson— made their reputation in Deadwood Gulch.

vast amounts of it, was never a sure thing. Gold mining is a risky enterprise, as much a gamble as playing a roulette wheel. Yes, some get rich quickly, but the odds run the other way. Veins of gold may peter out, accidents may destroy the mine, too much capital or too little may be invested, labor conflicts may cripple the mining, inflation or deflation may make profits vanish.

In 1891 Colorado would see another gold rush. It happened at Cripple Creek, on the shoulder slopes of Pike's

Over one hundred years after the discovery of the richest gold lode in the Western Hemisphere, the Homestake Mine in South Dakota is still in operation.

Peak, where Bob Womack, a part-time cowboy, hit pay dirt. This time, adding to the usual gold seekers, there would come a flood of men thrown out of work by the depression of 1893. Nearly 500 banks and 15,000 businesses failed. Millions of people struggled to hold off starvation. Maybe Colorado would change their luck?

A gold rush is a gold rush. Yes, but a new class of miners developed during the rushes of the latter 1800s. Call them professional prospectors. From all over the world they came running to every new rush, burning with the gold fever, always hopeful, rarely successful. In the accounts of gold rushes, you often see the same names popping up. Here's the man in California, again in the Black Hills, now in Australia, then in the Yukon, South Africa, Brazil. . . . The corporate seizure of gold mining drove such men away. They looked for new goldfields, for smaller rushes, where they could start again from scratch, hopeful that their own energy and labor might someday make them rich. Really rich.

It did, for some. Gold created at least thirty millionaires. The first and best-known was the carpenter W. S. Stratton. When he made his first million, he sold out his holdings for another $11 million. He gave much of his wealth to all kinds of causes and people in need.

By 1916 Cripple Creek's gold production had reached a total of $340 million as valued at that day's gold price; at today's price it would come to billions.

In the Yukon Territory of northwest Canada, close by the Alaska border, gold was discovered by the son of an American forty-niner. The date was August 12, 1896. He found it on the Klondike, a small stream that enters the Yukon River from the east at Dawson. The early prospectors became wealthy. Newly rich, they hurried away to spend their gold and glory in it. When one group headed back to civilization, their passenger ship carried so much gold the decks had to be reinforced. Leaving ship in Seattle or San Francisco, they became instant celebrities.

Headlines reported their ship carried a ton of gold (it was really two tons) and the public went mad. A million Americans made plans to rush to the Klondike; about a tenth of those actually set out, and perhaps 40,000 made it to Dawson. And how many struck it rich? Maybe 1 percent of them. There were many paths to the Klondike goldfields. The trails up were hellish going for the inexperienced, with mountain snows as deep as 12 feet. Bringing in a year's supplies for one miner took fifty trips up the Chilkoot Pass, each requiring six hours to complete, over a period of many weeks. Many gave up and turned back, if they didn't commit suicide or die of the hardships.

Page one of a pamphlet issued by the SooLine railway during the Klondike gold rush of 1898 (left). A party of gold seekers sets out from Edmonton, Canada, for the goldfields of the Klondike (above)

The Klondike rush was brief, following the pattern of almost all gold rushes, ancient and modern. After a few years the lone diggers gutted out the easiest parts of the gold deposits. Then in came the money men with the heavy machinery needed to do the rest of the job. Just as the Klondike faded out in the summer of 1899, another gold rush got under way in Nome, Alaska. Located along the Bering Sea, it was much easier to get to.

Like so many gold towns, Nome became a hive of greed, corruption, and violence as the human tidal wave from outside hit the beach. The sheriffs were all ex-convicts, the jail was a private and profitable domain, robbery was in full swing, elections were dishonest, and so was the court.

When the alluvial gold ran out, corporate mining took over. Some men found jobs in the big mines, while some, like tenant farmers, worked other people's claims in return for a share of the gold they found.

In the Klondike and Alaska, one historian says, the peak of the gold rush movement was reached. "Never again would the attraction be quite so powerful to such a variety of people or to so many."

From Australia to South Africa

A veteran of the California gold rush who failed to make good was the man who started the great Australia gold rush. While digging in California, Edward Hargraves noticed the rock-bearing gold was much like the rock he knew so well in his native Australia. Why not see if his luck would improve back home? It did: In 1851 he found gold in New South Wales, in the southeast corner of Australia.

Australia—call it the smallest continent or the largest island in the world—at that time was a land of sheep ranchers and convicts. Criminals in Britain were deported 16,000 miles to the penal colony on the far side of the Pacific. The convicts made up a majority of the mostly rural society. They worked as farm laborers or servants.

When the gold rush began, people of every class in Britain no longer thought of going to Australia as a terrible punishment. Overnight it became the land of opportunity.

Australian workers deserted the cities to dig in the mines, and so many sheep tenders quit the ranches that the owners had to import new ones from Scotland. The greatest number of outsiders came from Britain. But America contributed a large share too. So did China, with more going to Australia than had migrated to California.

At first the prospectors reaped "free gold"—that is, nuggets found in the streams near the surface, or even lying on the ground. Such amazingly large nuggets turned up that they were given names, like "Welcome Stranger." That one, weighing 2,285 ounces, was said to be the largest single chunk of gold ever found.

But after the surface gold was skimmed, it took much harder labor to reach the gold deeper down. The British crown controlled the gold and charged for a license to dig it out. A miner's license gave him the right to work an area of only 144 square feet. It forced him to dig deep vertical holes, through soil or rock, going as far as 200 feet down if he hoped to do well.

With so many difficulties, a few men would band together

Miners disputing a claim in the Australian goldfields.

on a claim to remove the earth. After shoveling or winching it up, the miners washed it for traces of the mineral. And by using the same methods used everywhere—the sluice, the cradle, the rocker, the long tom. Most of the diggers were young single men, though sometimes whole families worked the diggings. Children of six, eight, ten worked alongside their parents in the creeks or in the shafts. (There was no compulsory school in those days.)

The men in the camps entertained themselves, often with music. German miners formed choral groups or orchestras, Czechs organized bands, Scots skirled their bagpipes. Professionals came in too, for the goldfields promised good box office. Minstrels in blackface toured from America, and so did Shakespeare's plays, performed by the famous American actor Edwin Booth. Despite the shortage of women, men visited dance halls, which could supply only a few partners for the forty or fifty miners who came. One observer wrote, "It struck me as a queer sight to see hairy-faced men in pea jackets, and long boots, with pipes in their mouths, dancing together. . . ."

More fortunes were made out of the gold rush by business people than by miners. They supplied the food, clothing, tools, entertainment, transportation by land or sea. Whatever the miners needed or wanted, someone was sure to come up with it, for a fat price.

Sadly, the Chinese suffered persecution in Australia too. Yet their numbers increased steadily, from 2,000 in 1854 to 17,000 a year later. The government laid a heavy entry tax upon them, as well as many anti-Chinese laws. Twice there was bloody rioting against the Chinese.

By 1860 in eastern Australia the diggers gave way to the mining companies. The gold camps became permanent towns and cities. Gold mining was no longer a personal adventure but a major Australian industry.

In the 1880s another gold rush struck Australia, this time in the remote western part. It drew from the east many miners whose luck had failed them. They found Western Australia a desolate land. There was little vegetation and almost no water. In one goldfield the miners had to walk seven miles every day for water. Clouds of insects drove men mad if the heat didn't kill them first. And once again the lone miner would be displaced by big business.

In the same decade that gold was found in Western Australia, gold and diamonds were discovered in South Africa. Three elements came together with profound effect upon South Africa's history. The first was nature's unmatched deposits of wealth beneath the soil. The second was the financial skill and lust for profit of the Europeans; and the third was cheap black labor. Combined, they would remake South Africa entirely.

Back in the 1600s Europeans had opened up a frontier on

the southern tip of the huge continent, much as they had in North America at about the same time. The Dutch settled at the Cape of Good Hope as a way station for their trade with Asia. The white colonists—soon British as well as Dutch—expanded their areas slowly at first. They were often brutal, killing or enslaving the black people. The blacks fought back against the white invaders of their land. But by the late nineteenth century the whites' superior military technology gave them control of almost all of what is now known as South Africa.

It was cheap black labor, drawn from throughout southern Africa, that made possible the growth of the immense mining industry. The workers came from dozens of different tribes, speaking many different languages. The mine owners wanted to hire people of many different tribes and languages in order to reduce the danger of their getting together to organize. Within ten years of the discovery of gold nearly 100,000 Africans were working in the gold mines. Today it is close to half a million. And billions of dollars are being made—by white Randlords, as they are called—out of the gold they mine.

The goldfields run underground along a 350-mile arc,

with Johannesburg at its center. The area proved to contain the largest deposits of gold on earth. But it is not alluvial and close to the surface, to be scooped up easily. The ore is far beneath the rock, sandwiched between quartz rock overlaid with granite. It appears in the faintest and thinnest of layers. A ton of ore contains only a third of an ounce of gold, perhaps even less. For a few years it appeared no one could make a profit out of such mining. But then three scientists in Scotland developed a cyanide process to extract the yellow metal from crushed rock. The South African mines took it up, and by 1900 they were the world's largest gold producers.

Of course it took costly equipment and capital on a grand scale to recover gold from the immense but low-grade deposits. A deep South African mine could cost $500 million to $1 billion to bring into production, and it could be several years before an ounce of gold was taken out. The mines were soon in the hands of a syndicate of six giant interlocking corporations.

The higher-skilled and better-paying jobs were taken over by experienced white miners most of whom came from overseas. They formed a white trade union to protect their control of the better jobs and to resist attempts by management to lower labor costs by using blacks in their place or by encouraging immigration. Thousands of Chinese had been imported to work in the mines, but the white miners gradually drove them out of the industry.

Struggles for control of the mineral wealth and of political power led to wars between those of British descent and the Afrikaners, who were mostly of Dutch origin. The British gained control of the government for half a century, then in 1948 lost out to the Afrikaners.

It takes enormous effort to mine gold profitably. South Africa provides an example. At one point its 45 producing mines employed over 250,000 men working deep in the earth. Their labors produced about 25 million fine ounces of gold per year. That's about 780 tons. To get that gold, the miners dug out and lifted to the surface over 80 million tons of rock. You could put that whole year's output of gold into one truck. Except that the truck couldn't bear the concentrated weight, for gold is one of the heaviest of metals.

Workers, often called human moles, follow the path of a compressed air drill in the Crown Mine, Johannesburg, South Africa, during the late nineteenth century.

But no matter who was in political power, gold mining dominated the South African government as well as the economy. The government acted as though what was good for the mining corporations was good for the whole society. Gradually, the government clamped down upon the blacks with a system of laws that regulated their movements and brought them under harsh industrial control. Blacks continually resisted low wages and bad working conditions, but it always led to massive police brutality on the side of the mine owners.

Under the rule of the Afrikaners, discrimination and segregation were built into a complete system of law called *apartheid*, meaning "separateness." The Afrikaners claimed it was God's will that South Africa should be a segregated country with blacks kept apart from and under the control of whites. By 1990 the system had divided the country so that 4.5 million whites, only one sixth of the population, had control over 87 percent of the country. Blacks were allotted only 13 percent of the land, divided into ethnic "homelands." Half the blacks lived in black townships bordering white industrial centers, where they worked but had no political rights, such as Soweto, on the edge of Johannesburg in the heart of the gold district.

The areas blacks were confined to by law furnished the migrant-labor supply for the gold mines. The Africans were not allowed to establish homes in the towns and cities. The families of the migrant miners had to stay in the so-called home-lands while their men were away in the mines on contracts from nine months to two years. The mine owners paid African labor at rates so low that their families could barely survive on the money sent home.

Now the blacks have their own National Union of Mineworkers. It is gradually helping to improve everything from wages and living conditions to safety. And its growing economic strength has given it more political influence too. It is struggling to end the migrant-labor system. It wants to replace it with a more stable, better-paid, and skilled work force able to live near the mines with their families. The union is a vital force in the battle to wipe out South Africa's apartheid system.

Because gold provides close to 50 percent of South Africa's earnings abroad, mining is the focus of intense scientific research. Mining engineers use the latest technology to expand the existing mines by new shafts plunging to even greater depths. One new shaft takes miners over 12,000 feet down into the earth, deeper than man has ever gone. Rock-cutting and hydraulic drilling tools are gradually replacing the use of explosives. They make mining a continuous

Black workers in a gold mine near Johannesburg, South Africa.

process: Before, everything had to stop for the daily blasting. And they reduce the need to bring waste to the surface.

Geologists are exploring for entirely new goldfields beyond the borders of the present ones. And computer-simulation techniques help to design the layouts of shafts and tunnels at great depths to try to avoid the rock bursts that cause disasters in the deep mines.

A hopeful trend toward improved racial relations is the arrival of new mine operators unconnected to the old giants. They operate on a small scale in reviving old mines. They seek to create an open, multiracial work force with small teams of two or three working together underground, and for the same pay.

TEN

Nightmare
for Native Peoples

*F*or untold generations the Makuna Indians lived in the rain forest of Colombia, in South America. Their small communities were self-sustaining and had little connection to the world of modern Colombia. Missionaries never came to them. They had no schools nor any shops. Few Indians could speak Spanish, the national language. They knew little about the Colombia they were supposed to be part of. To them, government was some powerful chief living in a remote place called Bogotá.

An ancient rhythm shaped Makuna life. Men hunted, fished, and cleared and burned trees to make room for their gardens. Women planted, tended, and harvested the crops, except for the two—coca and tobacco—that were always men's work.

Then gold was found, and the Indians collided with a strange new world. It happened on the Traira River, which runs between Colombia and its neighbor to the east, Brazil. In the early 1980s *barranqueros*, as prospectors are called, began mining gold on the Brazilian side of the river. Soon they crossed over to the Colombian side. Within a few months gold miners moved in by river and trail.

The river was only a few days' walking distance from the Makuna people. By 1987 at least 5,000 miners were panning gold in the streams, scraping and lifting the topsoil, and digging tunnels into the hillsides. On their weekends off they jammed into the mining towns that sprang up in the middle of the forest. Government troops came in to drive out the armed guerrilla bands that tried to take control of the mining region.

But army or not, it is hard to keep order in mining towns at boom times. They grow without control. As more and more miners arrived (by 1990 there were about 200,000 in the country), more and more of the Indians' forest was chopped down. Excavating machines ripped up and gouged the streambeds. Wherever they went, the barranqueros left a devastated landscape, empty of vegetation and the animals the Indians hunted. The mercury they used to separate the gold polluted the rivers where the Indians fished.

Nevertheless, the Makuna chose to stay on their ancestral land. Even those young men who leave for a time to work outside return home to marry and live as their families always have. Some of the younger Makuna chose to dig gold. But the elders disapproved. The anthropologist Kaj Arhem, who has lived among the Makuna, says they believe "gold contains the light of the sun and stars, it is the 'stars of the earth.' Just as the sun and the stars are the visible manifestation of the ancestral beings of the sky world, gold is the sign of ancestral life on earth.

"Gold and the light it contains," he continues, "illuminate the Makuna world and allow the shaman [native healer] to see beyond the appearance of things into the world of spirits. . . . The elders say it is sacred; it belongs to the spirit of the hills and should be left where it is. According to the Makuna, the hills at the margin of the world form a protective wall against the force of evil on the outside. As miners penetrate into their world and take away their gold, the Makuna feel increasingly threatened."

The Makuna elders believe gold mining is a sign that the end of the world is coming. Their myths tell how the world of today had a convulsive beginning, replacing the old one that was destroyed. They fear that whatever new world may emerge from the ruins will have no place for the Makuna.

Strangers obsessed with finding gold have invaded many other parts of South America. Brazil led the way in the rebirth of gold mining. One day early in 1980 a ranch hand was bathing in a stream running down a low hill toward the Amazon River. He saw something glittering in the water, bent down, and picked up a piece of gold. Before a month passed, 5,000 people had turned that hill into a huge crater.

Soon after, at least 20,000 rushed into that same region, while a much greater number spread themselves over a large part of the vast Amazon Basin. The Brazilian government limits ownership of claims to plots only about 36 square feet, and miners must sell their gold to the government for 25 percent below world market value. In return, the army imposes law and order and provides medical services. Successful miners dig their tiny square plots 200 feet down. It is they who hire the poor peasants who come simply looking for jobs as laborers.

The miners of Serra Pelada, digging side by side on their small plots, produced a huge hole 600 feet deep and half a mile wide. It is a pit of red mud terraced on the sides. The laborers climb down to the bottom of the hole, fill a canvas sack with 40 or 50 pounds of wet dirt, and then carry it up to the top on a series of 100-foot handmade ladders. Up top, other workers sit in pools of water, cleaning the dirt and extracting the gold. Seen from above, the hole the size of a meteor crater looks like a gigantic anthill. Miners in constant motion, stopping, shoveling, stuffing the bags, climbing and descending the ladders (some falling and dying), and— different from a silent anthill—the steady sounds of cries and yells and a thousand tools.

A few workers might get a small percentage of the gold contained in the sacks. Most are paid daily according to the number of sacks they fill. The rate at one point was 15 cents a sack. But to starving peasants, it meant food.

Serra Pelada has suffered the disasters typical of other gold rushes. As the workers dug deep, the sides of holes often caved in, burying them alive in mudslides. In just one cave-in thirteen men were killed. A slum of lean-tos made up of black plastic and tree limbs grew up around the pit. No running water, no sewers. Malaria and other diseases have killed many workers. Prostitution soon became slavery, with bands of "businessmen" selling young women for $300 in gold dust. The workers themselves were often little better off than slaves. The land, too, was harmed. The mercury used in the recovery of gold destroyed the natural life of the rivers.

The way of life of Brazil's 220,000 Indians is threatened throughout the Amazon Basin by the drive for gold. In an attempt to save the Yanomani Indians, one of South America's last major tribes untouched by modern civilization, the Brazilian government in 1991 reserved a stretch of the Amazon rain forest as their homeland. The new reserve, coupled with a slightly smaller one across the border in Venezuela, permits the Indians to roam freely over nearly 70,000 square miles of wilderness.

The creation of the reserve overrode powerful mining interests. The Yanomani area is so rich in gold, tin, diamonds, and zinc that mining companies fought bitterly to prevent it. Now they can come in only if the Indian community and

Brazil's Indian protection agency both approve.

But hardly was the new law adopted when thousands of poor Brazilian gold miners, evicted from the Yanomani homelands, flooded across the border to the Venezuelan side of the Indian reserve. Within a year the mine companies they worked for had taken out an estimated $500 million in gold and diamonds, destroying, at the same time, the forests of an important watershed.

Enraged by the invasion, the Venezuelan military shot down planes carrying the miners, blew up illegal airstrips, attacked dozens of mining camps, burned down miners' barracks, and sank river barges equipped with suction pumps for mining. The Brazilians who avoided capture fled through the forest, heading for home.

The cross-border migration and the violence it roused were a sign of what may happen in the ten South American nations that share land borders with Brazil. The grinding poverty of the people in Brazil's northeast region will continue to lead many thousands to cross the Amazon's unmarked national borders in search of a living in the gold mines or other industries of those countries.

The saddest evidence is found in Peru. Thousands of children, as young as twelve, leave their homes every year in the hope of making a fortune by panning for gold in the Amazon region. The agents of mining companies recruit them in the Andean villages. But instead of finding great wealth, they enter a nightmare of exploitation. They work a ten- or twelve-hour day for the equivalent of $2.60. Standing in ankle-deep water, they hose down rocks and sand to wash out the gold, or they haul rocks, dig out hillsides, push wheelbarrows. The mine owner feeds his child laborers rice, potatoes, yucca root, and water. At night the children sleep in the open. In a few months, undernourished and overworked, many fall sick. Children fired because they become too weak to work are often not paid for the time they have already put in.

In such mining towns there is no public sanitation. Drinking water comes from streams into which the local sewage is dumped, and the children bathe in the same water. Many die of tuberculosis, malaria, and parasites because no money is provided for medicine.

For more than twenty years now Peruvian boys, and some girls too, have been working in the goldfields. In some places half the workers are boys under eighteen. No one knows the total number of children, but there are at least several thousand. Peruvian law bans using children for heavy labor, but the law is ignored. In many places the mine owner takes away the children's travel documents, in effect making them captives.

Gold—the dream of fortune hunters—has been a nightmare for the native peoples.

ELEVEN

What's It Worth?

Gold has played a part in the financial affairs of the world for at least 5,000 years. Throughout history gold has kept its value. It became the yardstick of the money system. The value of other currencies was tied to it. When people know they can exchange a certain number of silver or bronze or copper coins for a gold coin, they are willing to accept such coins. The same goes for paper money—the dollar, for instance. The dollar in itself has no worth at all, except for the tiny cost of its paper and ink.

To grasp the difference between two concepts—value and worth—helps you to see why gold has served as money all this time. Why does anything have value? Because people want it, demand it. If they don't want something, it hasn't any value.

But worth? If something has durable properties within itself, then it has worth. That's why gold has worth as well as value: For even as a raw chunk of yellow metal, it has artistic and industrial uses. But a dollar bill? Remove all the ink from it, and it's worth nothing.

As the heart of any money system, gold has many advantages. It's easy to transport, to store, and to subdivide. It can be readily recognized. It's hard to destroy. It lasts a long time without changing shape. It's hard to counterfeit. And it's scarce enough in the earth so that new supplies aren't constantly pouring into the market to upset the stability of its value.

You often hear about a "gold standard." That is a monetary system in which the value of currency is defined by a fixed quantity of gold. The American dollar, or the British pound, is held to be worth a specific amount of gold. Paper currency is freely changeable into gold, and both might circulate as money. If a country is on the gold standard, it has to hold stocks of gold in some safe place in order to back up its paper currency and meet its obligations.

Bars of gold inside a vault.

In the eighteenth and nineteenth centuries the gold standard gradually became the supreme monetary system of the major powers. Great Britain, the foremost trading and industrial nation, was on the gold standard for 200 years. At the Royal Mint the price of gold was set at an official value. In the 1870s many other countries began to adopt the British gold standard. But during World War I the nations at war dropped the standard because they wanted to use their stocks of gold to buy munitions and supplies. In 1934 President Franklin Roosevelt decreed $35 an ounce, and that standard lasted for almost four decades. Sometimes nations got together to fix the price of gold, making it easier to settle international debts. At other times, the price of gold has floated, that is, varied by market conditions. In the 1980s gold climbed to $850 an ounce, and then tumbled back to under $300.

Some people buy gold to make money, speculating that the future price of gold will be much higher. Others accumulate it to keep what money they have. Nervous about changing national or international conditions—inflation, taxation, famine, depression, revolution, war, etc.—they hang on to gold because they expect it to keep or increase its value.

You can see the point when you realize how trust in paper as money can drop badly. The U.S. dollar, for example, has slipped in relationship to gold. In 1971 a dollar was worth 1/35 of an ounce of gold. Three years later, it was rated at only 1/198 of an ounce. Which means you paid $35 to buy an ounce of gold in 1971, but $198 to buy the same amount in 1974.

A *huge amount of gold is in the hands of hoarders. Some estimate the value runs into many, many billions of dollars. There are people who bury gold in their backyards. The Germans pile up gold coins. So do the French, who like to keep it in small bars of gold as well. In India people collect gold jewelry. The Swiss encourage hoarding by placing small bars of gold in their children's Christmas stockings. Of course, it's only a small minority who have the means to buy the gold and hang on to it.*

The biggest gold treasury in the world is in the Federal Reserve Bank in New York. Thousands of tons of gold bars sit deep in its vaults below ground. Many nations besides the United States keep some gold there, letting the bank act as custodian. If country A wants to make a gold payment to country B, a lift truck moves the gold bars from A's cubbyhole to B's, and a computer records the changes in their accounts. Rarely does a gold transfer require shifting the metal from the bank to some remote place.

This may sound foolish, looked at in one way. Picture miners digging gold in deep holes in far corners of the earth, so it can be transported to another part of the world, where it is reburied in another deep hole, especially dug to receive it.

But does this mean gold is a useless metal? Far from it.

TWELVE

Many Uses, Many Pleasures

"Nothing is as good as gold."

That's often said by people who invest in the precious metal.

But gold has far more uses than that. Earlier we noted that no other metal is as good for a wide variety of industrial uses. It does not rust, tarnish, or corrode, and it is more adaptable for varied uses than any other metal. That's why in home computers and TV sets gold bonding wire filters electricity through integrated circuits. On undersea cables and in satellites, the connectors and switches have gold plating to guarantee endurance and reliability. In office buildings gold-coated windows keep the tenants cool, cut the air-conditioning bills, and save energy. When the astronauts soar into space, gold's reflective ability is used on the shields that are critical to life.

Integrated circuits are basic to the design of many things we use or rely on today, from video recorders to space-flight equipment. Those circuits use hairlike gold wires for the microelectronic webs that span the surface of the silicone chips. Gold is so pliable that this process of miniaturization requires only a wisp of gold for the integrated circuits and the printed circuit boards.

Gold plating has innumerable uses. Technology has taught us how to apply it to everything from costume jewelry to watch cases and watchbands, cigarette lighters, pens and pencils, spectacles, medals, bracelets, and bath taps. Liquid gold comes into play for ceramic and label designs. Gold thread brightens the saris women wear, and gold leaf gilds the domes of government buildings, brightens the ceilings of Japanese temples, and adorns the statues of the Buddha. There are new techniques to give a soft gold tone to cutlery by plating stainless steel in a bath of gold-cobalt or gold-iridium.

Physicians too have found applications for gold. For

rheumatoid arthritis they may inject a soluble gold-salt solution into the muscles, or they may prescribe a gold compound to be taken orally to avoid side effects of injected gold. In India, Hindu medicine prescribes gold preparations for certain conditions.

In dentistry, gold has been used for many centuries both to restore teeth and to splint teeth together or splint in appliances to replace missing teeth. Human remains found by archeologists in ancient Egyptian tombs of 2500 B.C. show attempts to stabilize decayed teeth by the use of gold wire. Around 500 B.C. the Etruscans in Italy used soldered gold bands as a bridge to hold teeth taken from animals together with the patient's own teeth. At about the same time the Phoenicians in North Africa were using gold wire to brace teeth.

Because gold does not corrode in the mouth and doesn't cause allergic or hypersensitivity reactions, dentists considered it an almost ideal material to work with in filling tooth cavities. They could easily hammer or stretch the malleable pure metal. Modern technology, however, using rotary instruments, led to alloying dental gold with other metals to increase its hardness and make it more durable.

In the United States, much more gold is used in the arts and crafts than in industry. The rest of the world is said to use even more, perhaps three or four times as much gold for such purposes. Gold was made into ornaments as early as 3000 B.C. The poet Homer mentions it. The art of the goldsmith is closely linked to those of the jeweler, enameler, sculptor, engraver. It was first worked by a hammering method—goldbeating, the craft is called. Gold was pounded into thin sheets called leaf. Look at medieval illuminated manuscripts displayed in museums or reproduced in books to see how they gleam with gold leaf. And it is still widely used for decorative purposes.

Goldbeating begins with a small ingot, cast from gold alloyed with small amounts of silver and copper. After several steps, it ends with leaves reduced to a translucent thinness. They are so delicate that your breath will move them. Gold leaf is applied in gilding and ornamental designs for lettering, edging on paper, wood, ceramics, glass, textiles, and metal.

The earliest surviving gold work is Egyptian jewelry. By 3000 B.C. it played an important role in that civilization. A wall painting in one tomb depicts a metal worker using tongs and a blowpipe to anneal gold, that is, to heat it so it can be softened. The quality of the work is visible in the wealth of gold ornaments found in the tomb of Tutankhamen. For such rich production of jewelry two conditions are needed: wealthy patrons and a taste for luxury.

During the 1870s Heinrich Schliemann discovered in the ruins of ancient Troy the greatest archeological treasure ever found: a large hoard of gold jewelry dating about 2500–2300 B.C. The fabulous treasure included thousands of gold objects: crowns, coins, rings, bracelets, goblets. By 2000 B.C., Minoan goldsmiths on the Mediterranean island of Crete were doing advanced filigree work in gold. Minoan culture spread to the mainland of Greece, dominated at that time by the city-state of Mycenae. When its royal tombs were excavated, refined goldwork in the form of vases, cups, jewelry, and weapons came to light.

Greek craftsmen who migrated throughout the Roman world brought their skills as goldsmiths. Their ingenuity was remarkable. They could cast the gold, anneal it, form it, fasten the parts together, polish the surface, and finish the jewelry with decorative details. And all this without machinery

RIGHT: *A Theban fresco from ancient Egypt, 18th dynasty, shows goldsmiths at work.*

Scene in the workshop of a Parisian goldsmith of the sixteenth century.

and with only the simplest of tools.

In the Middle Ages the monarch and the church were the principal patrons of the arts. Gold jewelry was produced mainly in royal and monastic workshops. But by the thirteenth century, as their crafts became more widespread, a system of independent guilds of goldsmiths had become established in the capital cities of Europe. The Worshipful Company of Goldsmiths, still flourishing as a guild, was founded in London before 1180. Its patron saint is St. Dunstan, a medieval monk. Sometimes goldsmiths won great reputations. The Italian goldsmith Benvenuto Cellini was famed for such precious objects as the gold-and-enamel salt-cellar he designed for Francis I of France. He played a major role in setting the artistic and technical standards that leading goldsmiths have tried to maintain ever since.

In the eighteenth century goldsmiths turned more practical, creating decorative articles for use as well as display in palaces or middle-class households. A century later the Industrial Revolution began to influence techniques of working in metals. Goldsmiths became artist-businessmen, running workshops of designers and craftsmen. They adapted methods of mass production to meet the needs of a growing middle class.

Today the artist-goldsmiths have revived the skills of the ancient craft, heading away from the monotony of industrial methods of production.

As ancient as goldbeating is the art of weaving and embroidering with gold thread. One of the first mentions of gold thread occurs in the Bible. Describing the ephod—the official garment worn by a high priest—made for Moses' brother Aaron, Exodus 39:2–3 says: "And he made the ephod of gold, blue, and purple, and scarlet, and fine twined linen. And they did beat the gold into thin plates, and cut it into

Gold cup with four gazelles. From Iran, c. 1000 B.C.

Gold vessel ending in the forepart of a lion. From Iran, fifth century B.C.

wires [strips] to work it in the blue, and in the purple, and in the scarlet, and in the fine linen, with cunning work."

You find references to gold textiles in both the *Iliad* and the *Odyssey*. Weavers in ancient Babylonia and Assyria used gold threads, and from them the Persians learned their celebrated skills as weavers. Darius, the conquering Persian king, wore a war mantle with two golden hawks shown pecking at each other. When Alexander the Great marched into Asia, he found its royalty dressed in robes of gold and purple. The Romans used gold thread, some of their leaders wearing tunics made entirely of gold threads. Clearly the art of weaving and embroidering with gold passed from one ancient city to another, usually moving westward. In the Middle Ages Europe's royalty and the church's high dignitaries used cloth of gold for state and ceremonial robes as well as for costly wall hangings. Tapestry and even carpets might be woven with gold thread.

The Western Hemisphere was rich in gold and other metals, but the Indians used metal to a modest degree. The craftsmen of the city-states of Mexico were highly skilled in the working of gold, silver, and stone. We saw (Chapter 6) what magnificent craftsmen the Inca were, and how Pizarro destroyed their work when he reduced it to raw metal. Some of that gold, shipped to Spain, was made once again into beautiful objects, this time to decorate the homes of wealthy nobles and merchants. All for "the greater glory of God and man," as the Spanish put it.

Masks—sometimes shaped of gold—were worn by Native Americans in North, Central, and South America before the arrival of the Europeans. Children, shamans, dancers, ballplayers put on the fantasy face coverings for many occasions. Masks were worn to help win battles, to conceal identities, and for plain fun at great parties. They depicted fierce beasts, the gods, human skulls, or the artists' wild imaginings. Many were worn for celebrations, performances, and burials. Others were designed as jewelry or as plaques to be fastened to buildings or tombs. Some were fashioned as helmet masks, to be worn as part of costumes that covered the entire body and made the wearer look like a whale, a duck, a parrot. In Peru the craftsmen of the period A.D. 600–1000 shaped sheets of gold into human faces with tab ears and disk earrings.

The making of arms and armor throughout the world has often included the use of gold. The armorer, the swordsmith, and the gunsmith produced work of notable design and decoration, often intended more for display than actual combat.

Even back in the fifth century A.D., when nomadic chieftains swept over Europe, arms and armor were richly embellished to demonstrate wealth, rank, and power. The armor-clad knights of the age of chivalry and the perfumed courtiers of Louis XIV did the same. If you examine Islamic miniature paintings, you find warriors and princes clad in gilded armor. In Iran, Turkey, and India swords and daggers too were often decorated with gold. Japan's craftsmen made arms and armor for a thousand years, creating gold-inlaid weapons and suits of steel armor gleaming with decorative gold.

Today thousands of tons of gold are consumed every year in the making of jewelry. It is the cornerstone of the gold business. Most of it is bought for fashionable adornment and not for investment. The Japanese have gone beyond jewelry to create even more extravagant uses for gold. Business firms give favored customers 24-karat teapots, vases, chopsticks, or saki cups to celebrate big contracts. At a hot springs resort near Tokyo visitors can plunge into a tub made of pure gold. An art museum features a golden tea-ceremony room whose pillars and beams are covered with rolled gold and

LEFT: *Armor made of steel and gold for an English nobleman, George Clifford, 1580–85. It weighs 60 pounds.*

walls papered in gold leaf. The teapots and cups too are made of 24-karat gold.

In the Middle East, gold shops are social centers where customers can buy rings, bracelets, necklaces, and other gold items as they relax over tea or coffee. At a factory in Panama City craftsmen make copies of golden beetles, butterflies, crocodiles, frogs, and turtles fashioned by pre-Columbian Indians six hundred years ago, to be sold in American museum gift shops. They also use the lost-wax techniques to create golden replicas of orchids and African violets, cast from the flowers themselves. In Athens, jewelers re-create ancient gold jewelry found in the excavations of Crete and Mycenae.

Large amounts of gold often change hands at marriage. In Morocco a bride may wear a golden belt, in Saudi Arabia a lacelike embroidery of gold chain interwoven with small gold coins. In India a family's standing in the community is judged by the gold that is given as the bride's dowry in marriage. In the Middle East and along the coastal countries of North Africa, local factories shape gold coins or small bars of gold, which millions of people buy as a basic form of savings. They do not have or do not trust banks, saving plans, or stock markets and would rather hoard the gold in their homes.

India is one of the world's largest gold markets for just such reasons. Much gold is smuggled in to avoid government controls. Farmers put the profits of a good harvest into gold ornaments, not into banks. At least 300,000 goldsmiths scattered throughout towns and villages of India act as money-lenders, taking golden objects and giving cash when there is sickness in a family or a crop fails. No fuss, no paperwork—just a swift and simple transaction.

Much of the world's gold jewelry today is the product of machines, not craftspeople. One American factory specializes in rings. The wedding ring accounts for more gold consumption than any other piece of jewelry. Normally 14-karat gold wire, thick as a wooden match, runs into machines that spit out finished rings faster than the eye can follow. An Italian factory specializes in gold chains, with 500 chain-making machines, row on row, turning out glittering chains in an endless stream. A town in Germany has 900 small factories producing gold jewelry. The result may not be art, but mass production brings jewelry within the price range of people who otherwise might not be able to afford it.

In the story of gold through the ages we can trace one quality of humankind: its great inventiveness. True, accident often led to the discovery of gold, but ingenuity has played a great role in devising techniques to locate the gold in the earth, to mine it, to process it, and to transform it into a myriad of objects for a myriad of uses, including the sheer pleasure found in looking at beautiful things made of gold.

The ingenuity is nothing new. We sometimes think it was beyond the capacity of the ancient peoples. But it rests on the innate imaginative power of individuals anywhere, everywhere, and in any time. Some of the superb gold objects made by the Inca people survived the destructiveness of the Spanish conquistadores. That the Inca were far more ingenious craftsmen than previously thought was demonstrated only recently. A scientist at the Massachusetts Institute of Technology, interested in ancient technologies, examined some Inca artifacts believed to be of hammered gold. Her analysis showed that they had been gilded with an incredibly thin layer of gold using a chemical technique that achieved the quality of modern electroplating. No one before this had thought the Inca had the scientific knowledge to create so subtle a technology.

So human ingenuity has proved boundless throughout history. That is but one conclusion to be drawn from the story of gold. The powerful appeal of the glittering metal has led people to explore every corner of the earth for it, to risk their lives and fortunes to mine it, to trade it, mint it, invest in it, to steal and even kill for it. Yes, and to create beautiful works of art out of it.

Gold has been a durable element of human existence for many thousands of years. It is likely to go on being valued beyond any time we can foresee.

APPENDIX

Table of Weights

The most familiar weight system in the United States is measured in *pounds avoirdupois*; however, precious metals are most often measured in *pounds troy*, which are about 20% lighter and are broken down differently. The differences are not critical to this text, but you may want to know how they relate to each other. (The weight of a grain is constant.)

Avoirdupois (abbreviated avdp.)	Troy (abbreviated t.)	Metric Weights
ton		**metric ton**
2,000 pounds		2,000 kilograms
32,000 ounces		1,000,000 grams
.907 metric tons		2,205 pounds avdp
pound	**pound**	**kilogram**
16 ounces	12 ounces	1,000 grams
7,000 grains	5,760 grains	2.205 avdp.
453.6 grams	373.24 grams	
ounce	**ounce**	**gram**
480 grains	480 grains	.035 ounce avdp. or
31.103 grams	31.103 grams	15.432 grains
grain	**grain**	**carat***
.0648 grams	.0648 gram	.2 tram or 200 milligrams
		.007 ounce

*Carat, a unit of weight, should not be confused with karat, a unit of purity.

Bibliography
and
Source Notes

My principal sources are listed alphabetically. Then, chapter by chapter, those sources relied on for the content of that chapter are singled out, using the last name of the author.

❦ *Bibliography* ❦

Angier, Bradford. *Looking for Gold*. Harrisburg, Pa.: Stackpole, 1980.

Arhem, Kaj. "Dance of the Water People," in *Natural History*, January 1992.

Bigler, David L., ed. *The Gold Discovery Journals of Azariah Smith*. Salt Lake City, Utah: University of Utah, 1990.

Bloch, Marc. *Land and Work in Medieval Europe*, "The Problem of Gold in the Middle Ages," pp. 186–218. New York: Harper, 1967.

Bohannon, Paul. *Africa and Africans*. New York: Natural History, 1964.

Braudel, Ferdinand. *Capitalism and Material Life, 1400–1800*. New York: Harper, 1973.

———. *The Mediterranean*, Vol. I. New York: Harper, 1973.

Cash, Joseph H. *Working the Homestake*. Ames, Iowa: Iowa State University, 1973.

Chernow, Ron. *House of Morgan*. New York: Atlantic Monthly, 1990.

Chijioke, F. A. *Ancient Africa*. London: Longmans, 1966.

Cipolla, Carlo M. *Money in Sixteenth Century Florence*. Berkeley, Calif.: University of California, 1989.

Curtin, Philip D., ed. *Africa Remembered*. Madison, Wisc.: University of Wisconsin, 1968.

Davidson, Basil. *A History of East and Central Africa to Late 19th Century*. New York: Anchor, 1969.

———. *A History of West Africa to 19th Century*. New York: Anchor, 1966.

Elliott, J. H. *The Old World and the New, 1492–1650* London: Cambridge University, 1970.

Fatout, Paul. *Meadow Lake Gold Town*. Bloomington, Ind.: Indiana University, 1969.

Ferkiss, Victor C. *Africa's Search for Identity*. New York: Meridian, 1967.

Fetherling, Douglas. *The Gold Crusades: A Social History of Gold Rushes, 1849–1929*. Toronto: Macmillan, 1988.

Green, Timothy. *The Prospect for Gold: The View to the Year 2000*. New York: Walker, 1987.

Hoffman, Herbert, and Patricia F. Davidson. *Greek Gold: Jewelers in the Age of Alexander*. New York: Brooklyn Museum, 1965.

Holliday, J. S. *The World Rushed In: The California Gold Rush Experience*. New York: Simon & Schuster, 1981.

Honour, Hugh. *Goldsmiths and Silversmiths*. New York: Putnam, 1971.

Jeeves, Alan H. *Migrant Labor in South Africa's Mining Economy,*

1890–1920. Montreal and Kingston, Ont.,: McGill–Queen's University, 1985.

Keesing, Nancy, ed. *Gold Fever.* Sidney, Australia: Angus & Robertson, 1967.

Kelly, Brian, and Mark London. *Amazon.* San Diego, Calif.: Harcourt, 1983.

Meltzer, Milton, *Slavery: A World History.* New York: Da Capo, 1993.

Morrell, William P. *The Gold Rushes.* Chester, Pa.: Dufour, 1968.

Parry, J. M. *The Discovery of the Sea.* Berkeley, Calif.: University of California, 1981.

Rensi, Ray C., and H. David Williams. *Gold Fever: America's First Gold Rush.* Atlanta, Ga.: Georgia Humanities Council, 1988.

Sprague, Marsha. *Money Mountain: The Story of Cripple Creek Gold.* Boston: Little, Brown, 1953.

Starr, Kevin. *America and the California Dream, 1850–1915.* New York: Oxford University, 1973.

Vicker, Ray. *The Realms of Gold.* New York: Scribner, 1975.

Wheatcroft, Geoffrey. *The Randlords.* New York: Atheneum, 1985.

Wilson, Mitchell. *American Science and Invention.* New York: Simon & Schuster, 1954.

Wolf, Eric R. *Europe and the People Without History.* Berkeley, Calif.: University of California, 1982.

WPA Writer's Project. *California: A Guide to the Golden State.* New York: Hastings, 1939.

❦ Source Notes ❧

To my knowledge there is no single volume that covers all the ground of this book. I wrote about whatever aspects of gold interested me, going to a variety of sources in search of facts and insights. Several of the books listed above—especially Fetherling, Green and Vicker—were useful in more than one chapter.

CHAPTER I

Gold's characteristics may be found in almost any encyclopedia or guide to mineralogy. Angier and Vicker are useful for ancient history and legends bearing on gold.

CHAPTER II

Anything the eminent French historian Braudel has published enriches the reader's knowledge and understanding of the past. He always goes far beyond the specialist to break down barriers between disciplines. His works provided background on barter, trade, and coinage. So did Vicker.

CHAPTER III

How placer and lode or vein mining is done is described in Angier. A detailed account of what it is like to mine deep in the earth is in Vicker. *The New York Times* for November 24, 1991, reported on how people today are schooled in prospecting for gold.

CHAPTER IV

Meltzer's world history of slavery has much on its use in the ancient world to mine gold and other minerals. See also Green, Honour, and Morrell.

CHAPTER V

For African history, both ancient and modern, I used Davidson's volumes, Chijioke, Bloch, Wolf, and Ferkiss.

CHAPTER VI

The story of the age of discovery tracks so many countries and cultures that at least twenty of the titles in the Bibliography came into play. The resulting chapter is a fusion of so many bits and pieces of material from so many sources that it would be fruitless to list them here.

C H A P T E R   V I I

Gold mining in the Brazil and Siberia of the nineteenth century is in Morrell, Braudel, and Green. The much-neglected episode of the Georgia gold rush of the 1820s is covered in Rensi. Probably more has been written about the California forty-niners than on any other gold rush in history. Starr is excellent for placing it in cultural context, and the treasured WPA guidebook to California is chockful of entertaining anecdote and detail. Bigler provides firsthand evidence from a gold rush journal, and Fatout focuses on one gold town. Wilson deals with the technological aspects, and Fetherling and Holliday view the gold rush as social history.

C H A P T E R   V I I I

The twists and turns for post-'49 gold rushes in Canada and the United States are in Fetherling and Morrell. Sprague provides an account of the gold strike at Cripple Creek, and Cash of the Homestake mine.

C H A P T E R   I X

The contributors to Keesing's collection cover many aspects of Australia's gold fever. Fetherling, too, has much on Australia and is also helpful on South Africa. There are many studies of South Africa's immense goldfields. Jeeves covers the use of migrant black labor in the early history. Vicker and Wolf go into the use of apartheid to control labor and politics, and Wheatcroft offers fascinating portraits of the Randlords, the men who have dominated the production and marketing of South Africa's gold.

C H A P T E R   X

Latin America's modern history has been shaped—or misshaped—by European invaders ever since the arrival of Columbus. The studies of the effects of gold mining reflect it. The Arhem report on the Makuna of Colombia offers an anthropologist's observations. The Serra Pelada and other mines of Brazil are described in the greatest detail in Kelly, and also in Fetherling and Green. The most recent reports on the threat of mining to Indian life and culture come from *The New York Times* for August 26, September 17, October 17, and November 19, 1991, and February 16, 1992.

C H A P T E R   X I

Gold is tied tightly to the mysterious (for most of us) movement of money. Reading the business pages of the daily press, with their bewildering arrays of statistics on the rise and fall of markets, is much harder than following baseball statistics on the sports pages. Here I have tried to reduce the complex story of the gold standard and the buying and selling of gold to the simplest terms (in my shortest chapter!), leaning heavily on the experts. Angier, Vicker, Wheatcroft, and most of all Green, deserve thanks.

C H A P T E R   X I I

The uses to which gold is put in industry, the arts, and the crafts is described in detail or in passing in many books about these fields. I owe information on the application of gold to dentistry to Dr.

Matthew Neary. Honour's work on the history of the goldsmith's art is excellent and lavishly illustrated in color. Green and Vicker are wide-ranging and full of helpful detail. Cipolla covers the minting of gold coins in the Renaissance. The Jewelers of America, a trade association, publish brochures on the work of their craft and industry. Elliott tells of the fate of the gold sent to Spain by Pizarro and other adventurers. *Time* magazine for September 23, 1991, was the source of the MIT analysis of Andean artifacts.

❧ Index ❧

❧ *About the Author* ❧

Milton Meltzer so enjoyed writing the story of *The Amazing Potato* (1992) that he turned at once from that lowly vegetable to the brilliant mineral gold. He has published over eighty books for young people and adults in the fields of history, biography and social reform, and has dealt as well with such odd topics as memory, names, the potato and now gold. He has written or edited for newspapers, magazines, books, radio, television, and films.

Among the many honors for his books are five nominations for the National Book Award. He has won the Christopher, Jane Addams, Carter G. Woodson, Jefferson Cup, Washington Book Guild, Olive Branch, and Golden Kite awards. Many of his books have been chosen for the honor lists of the American Library Association, the National Council of Teachers of English, and the National Council for the Social Studies, and the New York Public Library's annual Books for the Teen Age.

Born in Worcester, Massachusetts, Mr. Meltzer was educated at Columbia University. He lives with his wife in New York City. They have two daughters and two grandsons.